THE MAGPIE RETURNS

A LEGEND RISES FROM THE ASHES

IAN ROBSON & PAUL GILDROY
with a foreword by **BRIAN TURNER CBE**

CONTENTS

Foreword by Brian Turner CBE 8
Introduction by Ian Robson 10
Into the Inferno 12

Angels on Horseback 20
Aromatic Coconut Prawns 22
Baked Crab 24
Baked Halibut with Pea and Ham 26
Blackened Monkfish on Squid Ink Rice . . 28
Bouillabaisse 30
Breaded Brill Fillet with
Spanish Potatoes 32
Cheeky Pakoras 34
Classic Skate with Black Butter and
Hasselback Sweet Potatoes 36
Poached Cod with Parsley Sauce 38
Cod, Butter Bean and Chorizo 40
Coley with Mussel and
Potato Chowder 42
Coquilles St Jacques 44
Crab Crusted Halibut with
Beetroot Dauphinoise 46
Croque-Madame with a Magpie Twist . . 48
Dover Sole and Crab Paupiettes
with Hollandaise Sauce 50
Firecracker Prawns 52

Traditional Whitby Fish & Chips 54
Garlic King Scallop and Squid 56
Green Pepper Squid 58
Haddock with Garlic and Shallot 60
Hake with Mussel & Potato Korma 62
Halibut and Wild Mushroom Fricassée . . 64
Herby Cod Bake 66
Hot Cods 68
Kedgeree 70
Lobster Carbonara 72
Lobster and Queen Scallop Broth
with Potato Dumplings 74
Lobster Mac 'N' Cheese 76
Mackerel with Pomegranate
and Goats Cheese 78
Magpie Fishcakes 80
Monkfish and Sausage Casserole 82
Mushy Peas 84
Mussels and Chips 86
Oak Roast Salmon Fishcakes 88
One-Pot Hake 90

Oysters with Tomato and Caper	92
Pan-Fried Mackerel, Parma Ham and Asparagus	94
Pan Fried Skate Wing with Warm Pickle Salad	96
Piri Piri Mackerel	98
Prawn, Mussel and Crab Spanish Tortilla	100
Roast Cod with Langoustines, Borlotti Beans and Ham	102
Roast Monkfish with Creamed Brussels Gratin	104
Salmon Kiev 'Bon Bons'	106
Scallop, Cauliflower, Artichoke and Caper	108
Scallops with Beluga Lentils	110
Scallops with Black Pudding Hash and Beurre Blanc	112
Sea Bass with Piccalilli and Anchovies	114
Seafood Jambalaya	116
Seafood Paella	118
Seafood Linguini	120
Shellfish and Samphire Stir Fry	122
Smoked Haddock Rarebit with Confit Tomatoes	124
Smoked Salmon 'Sur Le Plat'	126
Smoked Salmon Soufflé	128
Sole Veronique	130
Southern Fried Oysters	132
Tempura Oysters with Pancetta and a warm Sherry Dressing	134
Tikka Spiced Mackerel	136
Whitby Crab Linguini	138
Whitby Crab Pate with Pickled Cucumber	140
Whitby Eggs Benedict	142
Whole Megrim Sole, Brown Shrimp and Wild Garlic Butter Sauce	144
Wild Sea Bass Ceviche	146
Wild Sea Trout Ceviche	148
Woof with 'Pasta Puttanesca'	150
Fish & Ships	154
Thanks	158

FOREWORD

BY BRIAN TURNER, CBE

I don't know how many times I visited Whitby as a lad but it seems like dozens. The family used to pile into the car, not a lot of room for mum, dad and four kids but at least we were going somewhere for the day. By the time we hit Pickering, boredom had set in, I mean, how many times can you play 'I Spy'! The climb up the hills onto the moors was more than welcomed by all especially as we could stop, get out of the car and stretch our legs and survey the marvellous view of The Devil's Elbow. Gorse, heather, bilberries (in season) and the numerous birds to be spotted meant we had a great time running around and exploring before seeing Fylingdales where dad would tell us nuclear bombs were kept to protect us from aliens and Russians. That shut us up for a while as did the story of the nearby Saltergate Inn, where a peat fire is said to have burned continually for 200 years, legend has it that it was first lit to cover up the murder of a customs man. It went out in 2007!

Then slowly but surely the coast comes into view and on arrival at Blue Bank at the top of Eskdale one can see the Abbey overlooking the mouth of the great river Esk, silhouetted against the sea and I swear that, when I rolled the window down, I could smell fish and chips!! Now of course whenever I am in that area of North Yorkshire one of my prime objectives is to visit the recently re-opened Magpie fish and chip restaurant, deli or take away, sometimes twice! As the Phoenix of ancient times and mythology the Magpie has regenerated itself to a bigger and even better fish and chip emporium and it's fab.

The late great Jane Grigson tell us in her book that the white fish authority says we have in the UK well over 50 different species of edible fish. The Magpie is ideally placed to prove the point. The fish market is literally opposite the restaurant and literally 50 yards away the availability of so many varieties of fresh fish is a chef and restaurateurs' dream. Ian and chef Paul use this to their great advantage with so many wonderful dishes on the menu along with a very descriptive list of fish for all to study. Last time I was in the Magpie I saw a wonderful version of the French Plateau de Fruits de Mer, so impressive and no need to take the trip to the French Riviera, where else can you get ultra-fresh seafood, local and delicious? Also listed are dishes for gluten free diets as well as great dishes for vegans, vegetarians and even a steak for meat eaters. The restaurant looks even more homely with its collection of small rooms looked after by the friendly lovely staff and I have to say I was so impressed with the wine list at super prices even to Yorkshire folk! Look at the Picpoul de Pinet Beauignac and the Sancerre. Great wines, great prices.

If I'm honest I only go to the Magpie for one thing and for me the extra-large cod and chips does it every time. Great batter crisp and brown, superbly fresh fish steamed to perfection and chips made from real local potatoes, all cooked in Yorkshire beef dripping.

What a way to spend the day, so I'm going to queue up now for takeaway fish and 'feneucks' as my dad called them, or to you and me, fish and chips, open with salt and malt vinegar only. Eating them whilst walking down Pier Road, surveying the wonderful Whitby harbour is one of life's great privileges – The Magpie has returned! X

INTRODUCTION

FROM IAN ROBSON

This book has seemed like a lifetime in the making.

It all started so well in early 2017, we made a start on the recipes, when we had a few put together we enlisted the services of an excellent local photographer who would come to the restaurant before service and photograph our efforts. This went on smoothly for a few weeks until suddenly our world was turned upside down. Come Summer, 2017, we had nowhere to cook, let alone take photos of finished dishes. This situation went on for 34 long weeks while we battled to get The Magpie returned to its former glory. Then when we finally reopened, all our energies were put into restoring our place in Whitby's culinary scene. Even though the majority of our team returned to us there were inevitably some new ones to train up to Magpie standard (not to mention the ongoing battle with our insurers, but that's a story for another day). The last thing we needed was the distraction of writing a cookery book. Eventually, things returned to a semblance of normality and we felt we could take steps towards finally completing the book.

So here it is, probably the most drawn out cookbook in history. Hope you enjoy it.

Ian Robson

INTO THE INFERNO
A LIFE'S WORK UP IN SMOKE (ALMOST)

It had been a long day. That's the way it always is on a bank holiday weekend and April 30, 2017 proved to be no exception. The visitors had come in their thousands as usual to Whitby, encouraged by the lovely late spring sunshine.

The Magpie Café can cope with more than 800 diners a day at full stretch and the staff are well-accustomed to handling the pressure when called upon. The queue outside was as long as ever, and we'd just had the added boost of a rave write-up in the *Sunday Times* by the food critic AA Gill, in what turned out to be his last-ever review.

I first became involved in the Café in the summer of 1971 as a tall thin dark haired youth (I'm still tall but not so thin or dark haired) and was well into my fifth decade there. The intervening years saw the Café transformed from a small seasonal local favourite to a year round visitor destination in its own right and a name known far beyond these shores.

I didn't know it then but the Magpie was about to hit the headlines again – but this time for all the wrong reasons.

It was my son Duncan who discovered smoke on the top floor as he was locking up after the restaurant closed that evening. I had a phone call from him just after I got home. I drove back there in the few minutes it took for the fire brigade to arrive.

Within minutes they had tackled the fire. We took stock of the damage. Apart from some damage to the Gents toilets on the top floor, we had got away with it quite lightly. The finger of suspicion pointed towards an electrical fault.

It looked like we faced a closure of two weeks, three at the most, while the damaged area was restored and the restaurant could open for business again. And above all, no-one was hurt. A sense of shock soon gave way to overwhelming relief. It could have been much worse. Unfortunately we were about to find out just how much worse it could be.

The fire brigade eventually handed the building back to us in the early hours of the morning, having checked it using sensitive heat-locating equipment to ensure that the fire was indeed extinguished. All appeared well.

We began the clean-up operation and staff who had turned up to work as usual rolled up their sleeves and joined in.

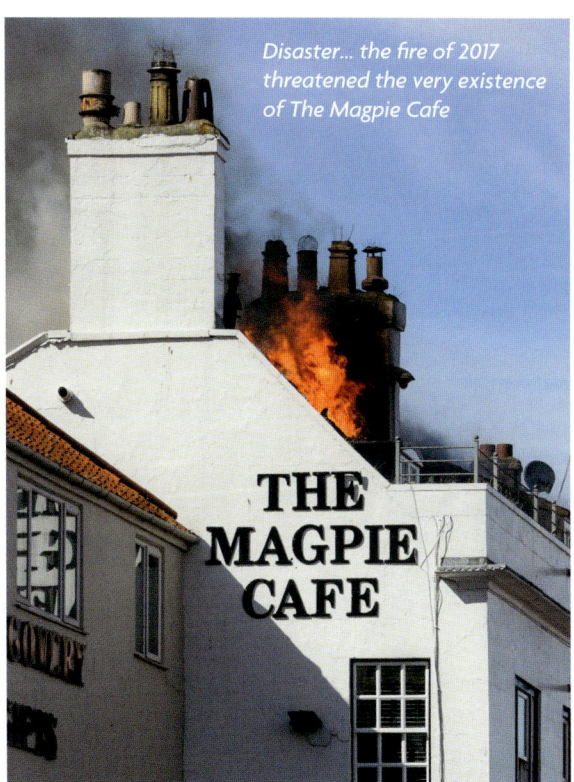

Disaster... the fire of 2017 threatened the very existence of The Magpie Cafe

At about 2.30, the call came from a passer-by. "I don't know how to tell you this," said the stranger, ominously, "but your roof is on fire".

After our initial disbelief, we looked for ourselves and saw the tell-tale smoke. The fire alarm triggered and we set about tackling the blaze with all our available fire extinguishers plus lots brought to us by our neighbouring businesses, 25 in total. We fought the fire for about 20 minutes, and had it all but under control, but were eventually beaten by the smoke.

It was then that things began to go badly wrong. Due to a computer problem in the emergency services control room it was some time before it was realised that no fire crews had been mobilised. The bank holiday weekend, in contrast with the customary rain and cloud, had been bright and sunny. A moderate breeze served to fan the flames, which within minutes were shooting high into the air above the 250-year-old listed building. The fire brigade had taken 40 minutes to arrive.

By the time the fire brigade came onto the scene, after the computer error and battling their way through the town centre bank holiday traffic, the entire roof was ablaze. Police cordoned off the area as crowds gathered at all vantage points on both sides of the river to gaze at the disaster unfolding before them.

Meanwhile I stood by on the quayside, powerless as the flames leapt ever higher. I was watching my life's work go up in smoke. There was no doubt in my mind that the Magpie Café would be utterly destroyed by the conflagration.

The fire brigade set to work with the hoses and a platform later came onto the scene. What seemed like millions of gallons of water were directed onto the roof, sweeping through the interior and wrecking everything in its path.

The fire raged into the evening, and it was not until the next day that we were able to enter the building again. The sight that greeted us was bleak indeed.

The entire interior would have to be replaced. But the structure itself had withstood the inferno. All that remained was to go through the formalities of the insurance claim. Or so I thought.

It soon became apparent that this would be far more than a mere formality. The insurers disputed the claim and that, in short, led to a legal battle which as I write this is still going on, with us yet to receive a single penny.

This was a further massive blow. One day we had a highly successful and nationally-renowned business, the next, it seemed, we had lost everything.

If we were to save The Magpie, we would have to do it alone.

Emergency family meetings were hastily convened to consider our options. Our bank, whilst sounding highly supportive, were

Aftermath... the extent of the damage was now clear. The next challenge was the mammoth task of restoring The Magpie to its former glory.

The daunting task of rebuilding begins.

very slow to react to our needs. Fortunately someone pointed us in the direction of Handelsbanken who were very proactive and great to deal with, just like banks used to be. And if we could raise enough cash, there was a chance the Magpie could rise from the ashes.

Savings accounts were emptied, pensions cashed and favours called in. To cover the £1.8 million cost of restoring the restaurant and a year's worth of lost takings would be a mammoth task, but at last it was achievable. As many staff as possible were retained, but instead of cooking and serving meals to visitors they pitched in with a determination to bring the place back to its former glory.

Over seven months is a long time for any business to be out of action, especially as the timing of events meant we would miss all the prime summer season.

There would be other things that we missed out on, most notably our place in the *Good Food Guide*, which we had held for the past 37 years. Thankfully we were reinstated in the 2019 Edition.

But the daunting task of bringing the Magpie back to life again had begun. There were new building regulations to take into account, scaffolding across the roof, and teams of construction workers everywhere.

By the end of the project, we had the place looking exactly as it was before the fire, but now smelling of new paint and carpets.

Eventually the moment we had waited for came along. After nearly eight months, we finally opened the front door to customers again and the entire restaurant was operational.

Fate had thrown the kitchen sink at us, but we were back.

As ever, we believe in looking forward, not back. So in that spirit I proudly present in this, our third book, 66 of my favourite seafood recipes for you to make at home.

See you at the Magpie soon.

ANGELS ON HORSEBACK

SERVES 4

16 shucked oysters
16 thin slices of pancetta
16 thin slices of French stick
Sweet smoked paprika
Rocket leaves
1 clove of garlic
Black pepper

For the mayonnaise
2 very fresh egg yolks
1 teaspoon English mustard
60ml white wine vinegar
300ml good quality vegetable or rapeseed oil
Squeeze of lemon juice
Salt to taste
Wholegrain mustard

METHOD

For the mayonnaise; Place the egg yolks, English mustard and vinegar into a food processor and blitz until well combined. Whilst the processor is still running slowly add the oil until the mayo is thick. Add salt and a squeeze of lemon juice, transfer the mayo to a sterilised jar and place into the fridge. (This can be stored in the fridge for up to seven days).

For the oysters; lay out each slice of pancetta and lay on one or two rocket leaves per slice. Lightly sprinkle on some smoked paprika and black pepper then an oyster on each slice of pancetta. Roll each oyster up in the pancetta and secure with a cocktail stick.

Heat a little oil in a pan. Add the oysters to the pan and fry until the pancetta is crispy all round. Place onto kitchen paper to drain.

Toast the slices of French bread. When browned, rub each slice with garlic.

Take the mayo from the fridge and mix through some wholegrain mustard. Place a good teaspoon onto each slice of bread and sit on an angel. Serve immediately.

AROMATIC COCONUT PRAWNS

SERVES 4

16-20 king prawn tails
2 banana shallots, finely sliced
2 red chillies, finely chopped
Half a thumb-sized piece of fresh ginger, grated
Half a fresh lemongrass stalk, finely chopped
3 spring onions, finely chopped
Juice and zest of 1 lime
400ml coconut milk
150ml double cream
1 tablespoon chopped coriander
Oil for cooking

METHOD

Heat a little oil in a pan and add the prawns. Cook over a high heat for 2 minutes.

Add the shallots, chilli, ginger, lemon grass and spring onion. Cook for a further minute and then add the juice and zest of the lime and the coconut milk.

Bring to the boil, moving the pan to mix the ingredients. Pour in the double cream and simmer for 3-4 minutes until the prawns are cooked and the sauce has reduced a little. Stir through the chopped coriander.

Serve in a bowl with slices of toasted bread.

BAKED CRAB

SERVES 4

200g white crab meat
200g brown crab meat
200g mascarpone
2 teaspoons Dijon mustard
2 tablespoons soured cream
1 small onion, finely chopped
1 clove of garlic, crushed

1 tablespoon Henderson's Relish
Half teaspoon smoked paprika
200g grated mature Cheddar
1 tablespoon fresh parsley, chopped
1-2 fresh green chillies, finely sliced
Fresh bread for dipping

METHOD

Cream the mascarpone, mustard and soured cream together, then add the onion, garlic, Henderson's Relish, smoked paprika, two thirds of the cheddar and parsley. Stir this through before adding the crab meat. Mix until well combined and then place into an ovenproof dish or split it into four individual dishes.

Sprinkle over the remainder of the cheddar and place the dish into a preheated (200°C/Gas 8) oven for around 20 minutes or until bubbling and golden on top.

Serve with grilled salmon and mustard dressed leaves.

BAKED HALIBUT WITH PEA AND HAM

SERVES 4

4 x 200g fillets of halibut
1 ham hock
1 medium onion, roughly chopped
500g frozen garden peas
50g butter
2 cloves of garlic, crushed
400-450ml ham stock (use the cooking liquor from the hock)
100ml double cream
Salt and pepper
Oil for cooking the fish

METHOD

For the ham hock; Placethe ham in a pan of cold water with onion, carrot, bay leaf and peppercorns. Bring to the boil and skim if necessary. Reduce to a simmer and cook for around 3 hours or until the meat will easily pull away from the bone.

Remove the hock and allow it to cool enough to handle. Strip all the meat off the bone. Pass the cooking liquor (ham stock) through a sieve and set aside.

For the pea purée; Melt the butter in a pan and add the onion and garlic. After a couple of minutes, add the peas and ham stock, bring to the boil and cook for 8-10 minutes.

Remove from the heat and blitz in a food processor until smooth. Add the cream and taste, adding more salt and pepper if needed.

For the halibut; Heat a little oil in a pan and carefully lay in each piece of fish, flesh side down. Cook for 3-4 minutes then turn the fish over. Add the stripped ham hock pieces and place the pan into a preheated oven (220°C/ Gas 8) for 6 minutes.

To serve; Sit the halibut on a spoon of creamy mash. Pour around the pea purée and finish with the ham hock pieces. Serve immediately.

BLACKENED MONKFISH ON SQUID INK RICE

SERVES 4

4 x 200g monkfish

For the rice
1 medium onion, finely diced
1 small fennel, finely diced
1 clove of garlic, crushed
500g paella rice
2 sachets squid ink (available at The Whitby Catch)
1 litre fish stock
1 tablespoon oil
Salt and pepper

For the spice
1 heaped teaspoon ground coriander
1 heaped teaspoon garam masala
Half teaspoon each of ground cumin, turmeric, hot chilli powder and garlic salt
Butter to brush the fish

For the raita
Half a cucumber, very finely diced
300ml natural yoghurt
1 tablespoon fresh mint, chopped
Half a green chilli, very finely chopped
Salt and black pepper

METHOD

For the raita; Place the cucumber in kitchen paper and squeeze any excess water out then simply mix with the yoghurt, mint, chilli and seasoning. Cover and chill (this can be made the day before).

For the rice; Lightly sauté the onion, fennel and garlic in the oil until softened. Add the rice, squid ink and fish stock and stir well. Bring to the boil then reduce the heat to a simmer, stirring often. Cook for approximately 20-25 minutes or until the rice is tender and most of the stock has been absorbed.

For the monkfish; Mix all the spices together, melt the butter and brush onto the fish. Coat the fish in the spice mix.

Heat a little oil in a pan and gently place the fish in it. Fry over a medium heat for approx 6-8 minutes, turning frequently.

To serve; Spoon some rice onto each plate and lay on a piece of monkfish. Finish with a spoonful of raita, a wedge of lemon and fresh herbs.

BOUILLABAISSE

SERVES 4

1 medium onion
1 bulb fennel
Half leek
3 cloves garlic
100ml vermouth or white wine
1 litre fish stock
Half teaspoon saffron
750g tomatoes, skinned, deseeded and roughly chopped
1 tablespoon tomato purée

200g fillet of gurnard, scaled and boned
200g fillet of sea bass, scaled and boned
200g fillet of monkfish, skinned
300g mussels
200g clams
8 raw king prawn tails, shelled and deveined
1 good sprig of thyme
1 tablespoon parsley, chopped
A little oil

METHOD

Finely slice the onion, fennel, leek and garlic. Heat the oil in a deep pan and add the vegetables. Lightly sauté.

Add the vermouth or wine, fish stock and saffron, tomatoes and purée. Bring to the boil, reduce and simmer.

Cut the pieces of fish so you have eight pieces of each variety and add to the soup along with the mussels, clams and prawns. Cover with a lid and cook for about 8-10 minutes.

Remove the lid and add the chopped herbs, check the seasoning and adjust. All the shellfish should be open (discard any that aren't) and the prawns should be lovely and pink.

To serve, share the fish and shellfish evenly into four large bowls. Pour over the liquor.

Serve immediately with lots of French bread.

> For this hearty fish soup we have used sea bass, gurnard and monkfish but any white fish will do.

BREADED BRILL FILLET WITH SPANISH POTATOES

SERVES 4

4 x 200g fillets of brill
100g plain flour
3 eggs, beaten
150g white breadcrumbs
2 lemons, skin and pith removed and cut into 8 slices
100g capers
Oil for cooking
50g butter
Salt and pepper

For the Spanish potatoes
400g baby potatoes
1 large onion, finely sliced
2 red chillies, finely chopped
3-4 cloves of garlic, crushed
2 x 400g tins chopped tomatoes
2 tablespoon oil
Salt and pepper

METHOD

For the Spanish potatoes; In a roasting tray, heat the oil and fry the potatoes until lightly browned. Add the sliced onion, chilli and garlic. Cook for a further couple of minutes. Add the chopped tomatoes, some salt and pepper, stir well and cover with a lid or foil, then place into a preheated oven (210°C/Gas 7) for about 20-25 minutes or until the potatoes are tender and the sauce has reduced slightly.

For the brill; Using three separate bowls from left to right place the flour (seasoned with salt and pepper), beaten egg and breadcrumbs.

Taking one fillet of brill at a time, lay into the flour, shake off any excess, coat with egg and then the breadcrumbs.

Pre-heat a pan with a little oil and one at a time lay in a fillet of brill, flesh side down and cook for about 4 minutes. Turn the fish over and cook for a further 4 minutes. Remove from the pan and place onto kitchen paper to drain. Place in the lower part of an oven to keep warm whilst you cook the other fillets.

Once all the fish are cooked, using the same pan add the lemon slices and cook for a couple of minutes to lightly colour, then add the capers and butter.

To serve, place a spoonful of Spanish potatoes on each plate, then brill fillet and sliced lemon, capers and butter.

CHEEKY PAKORAS

SERVES 4–6

400g cod or monk cheeks
200g gram (chickpea) flour
2 teaspoon ground turmeric
1 teaspoon cayenne pepper
1 red chilli, very finely chopped
2 shallots, very finely chopped
200ml ice cold water

For the marinade
Juice of 2 limes
2 teaspoon garam masala
1 tablespoon finely-chopped coriander
Salt and pepper
Sunflower or vegetable oil for deep frying

METHOD

For the fish; Mix together the lime juice, garam masala and coriander. Season well with salt and pepper then add the pieces of fish. Toss in the marinade, cover with clingfilm and place into the fridge for about an hour, turning the fish occasionally.

For the batter; Take a bowl and add the flour, turmeric, cayenne, chilli and shallot. Season with salt and pepper. Gradually whisk in the chilled water until the batter resembles double cream (you may need a little less or a little more water). Cover and place into the fridge to rest.

Heat the oil in a pan (the oil should not be more than half way up the pan) to around 175°C. Dip each piece of fish into the batter and then carefully into the hot oil. Deep fry for 6-7 minutes or until the batter is golden and crisp (this is probably best done in small batches). Drain on kitchen paper and serve immediately with minted yoghurt.

CLASSIC SKATE WITH BLACK BUTTER AND HASSELBACK SWEET POTATOES

SERVES 4

4 x 400g skate wings
Fish stock for poaching
Salt and pepper

For the black butter
200g butter
Juice of half a lemon
100g capers
1 heaped tablespoon of chopped parsley

For the potatoes
4 sweet potatoes
100g butter
Salt and pepper
Honey for basting
4 dessertspoons soured cream
1 spring onion, finely sliced

METHOD

For the potatoes; Make incisions into each potato approximately 2-3mm apart and three quarters of the way through the potato. Place these onto a baking sheet and brush generously with the butter, season with salt and pepper and place into a preheated oven (190˚C/Gas 7). Bake the potatoes for around 40-50 minutes basting them with honey every 10 minutes until cooked.

Heat the fish stock in a couple of large flat pans. When nearly boiling lay in the skate wings, thickest side facing up. Season with salt and black pepper and cover with a lid.

Poach the skate wings over a low to moderate heat for around 10-12 minutes or until the fish could be lifted from the bone (this is a good indication that the fish is cooked all the way through).

Whilst the skate is cooking, make the black butter by heating the butter slowly in a pan. After a while the butter will begin to froth and eventually will also begin to change colour (this is the milk solids in the butter caramelising). Once the butter is a hazelnut brown colour remove it from the heat and add the lemon juice, capers and chopped parsley. Shake the pan to mix thoroughly.

To serve, place the skate wings onto plates and spoon over the 'black butter' and serve with the hasselback sweet potatoes.

POACHED COD WITH PARSLEY SAUCE

SERVES 4

4x 300g fillets of cod, skinned and boned
4 shallots, finely sliced
50g anchovy fillets
150ml fish stock
500ml full cream milk
200ml double cream
Salt and pepper
2 tablespoon fresh parsley, chopped
50g plain flour
50g butter

METHOD

In a pan or deep tray large enough to hold all four pieces of fish, cover the base with a layer of shallots and anchovies on the bottom and place the fish on top. Season with salt and pepper. Pour in the fish stock and milk, Cover with a lid or foil, place over a low heat and gently simmer until the fish is cooked (it should look white and feel firm to the touch and will easily flake if pressure is applied).

Remove the fish and keep warm whilst you make the sauce.

To make the sauce; Put the milk back onto the heat and add the cream. Mix the butter and flour together to form a paste (this is what we call a beurre manié or uncooked roux). When the milk is hot, whisk in the flour paste and slowly bring to the boil. Simmer for a minute to cook out the flour. Finally add the chopped parsley, taste for seasoning and adjust if required.

To serve; Place each fish onto a plate and carefully pour over the sauce. Serve with boiled potatoes and seasonal vegetables.

COD WITH BUTTER BEAN AND CHORIZO

SERVES 2

2 x 250g cod loins
1 medium onion
200g chorizo
150ml chicken stock
1 x 400g tin butter beans
Flour for dusting
2 generous handfuls of fresh spinach
50g butter
Salt and pepper
Oil for pan frying

METHOD

Finely slice the onion and dice the chorizo. Over a medium heat, saute in a little oil until the onions are soft and the oils are coming from the chorizo. Add the chicken stock and butter beans and crank up the heat to bring to a boil. Reduce to a simmer and cook for 10 minutes.

For the cod; Season the flour with salt and pepper and roll the cod loin through it. Heat a little oil in a frying pan and carefully lay in the cod. Fry over a moderate heat, turning occasionally. This should take 8-10 minutes – the cod will feel firm and be golden brown in colour.

To finish; Add the spinach, butter and seasoning. Once the spinach has begun to wilt, toss the pan to mix with the beans and chorizo, taste and adjust the seasoning as required.

Finish with chopped parsley and serve.

COLEY WITH MUSSEL AND POTATO CHOWDER

SERVES 4

4 x 200g coley fillets (skinless)
8 slices proscuitto ham
500g mussels
4 shallots, sliced
1 clove of garlic, crushed
4 medium potatoes, diced
200ml fish stock
200ml milk
200ml double cream
25g soft butter and 25g flour mixed to a paste (beurre manié)

1 bay leaf
1 handful of parsley, chopped
Salt & pepper
Basil to finish

For the pesto
100g sun blush tomatoes
50g pine kernels
1 clove of garlic
1 handful of basil
150ml olive Oil

METHOD

To make the pesto simply blitz together all the ingredients and set aside for later.

For the chowder; Heat a little oil in a pan and add the shallots and garlic. Sauté until softened. Add the potatoes, bay leaf and stock, bring to the boil and cook for 12 minutes. Add the mussels, cover with a lid or foil and cook for a further 4-5 minutes or until the mussels have opened and potatoes are tender.

Remove the potatoes, mussels and Bay leaf from the pan and set aside. Once cool enough to handle, remove around half the mussels from the shells and combine with the potatoes and remainder of mussels.

Add the milk and cream to the pan of stock and bring to the boil. Whisk in the beurre manié and bring to the boil (this will thicken the sauce slightly but if it is too thick just add a little more cream). Return the mussels and potatoes to the pan, add salt and pepper to taste and finish with the chopped parsley.

For the coley; Wrap the prosciutto around the fish. Fry in a little oil over a high heat, seal the fish all round then place into a hot oven for 6 minutes. Lift the pan out of the oven and pour the pesto over the fish Return to the oven for a further 3 minutes.

To serve; Share the Chowder between 4 bowls and sit the Coley on top. Finish with fresh Basil.

COQUILLES ST JACQUES

SERVES 4 AS A STARTER

16 king scallops
500g peeled potatoes (use a floury potato such as Maris Piper or King Edward)
25g butter
50ml double cream
100ml white wine
50ml fish stock

1 clove of garlic
200ml double cream
100g butter
Parsley, chopped
Salt & pepper
75g grated Gruyère cheese
Parsley to garnish

METHOD

Peel and chop the potatoes, place into a pan of salted water and bring to the boil. Cook until tender, strain and mash with the 25g butter and 50ml double cream. Season to taste. Put into a piping bag and let cool enough to handle.

Pipe the potato into small rosettes on four individual dishes and place under a preheated grill to brown.

Whilst the potato is under the grill, put the wine and fish stock into a pan. Add the scallops, cover with a lid and poach for 3 minutes. Remove the scallops from the pan and keep warm. Bring the wine liquor to the boil. Add the garlic and cream, reduce a little and whisk in the butter and parsley. Remove from the heat.

Take the dishes from under the grill and plate the scallops four per portion. Pour over the sauce, top with the grated Gruyère cheese and place back under the grill until golden brown.

Remove from the grill and serve.

CRAB-CRUSTED HALIBUT WITH BEETROOT DAUPHINOISE

SERVES 4

4 x 200g halibut fillets
50g brown crab meat, chopped
80g white crab meat, chopped
3 slices stale white bread
50g butter
1 tablespoon parsley
Squeeze of lemon juice

For the beetroot dauphinoise
1 kg fresh beetroot
400ml milk
200ml double cream
2 cloves of garlic, crushed
1 tablespoon horseradish sauce
Salt and pepper
300g kale
Knob of butter
Oil

METHOD

To make the beetroot dauphinoise; Peel and very thinly slice the beetroot and layer into an ovenproof dish. Heat the milk, cream, garlic and horseradish together in a pan, season with salt and pepper and pour over the beetroot. Cover the dish with foil and place into a preheated oven (180°C/Gas 6) for 1 hour. Remove the foil and bake for a further 20 minutes.

For the crab crust; In a food processor, blitz the bread to a fine crumb, melt the butter in a pan and cook the breadcrumbs over a medium heat, stirring constantly until lightly toasted. Remove the pan from the heat.

Combine both crab meats, add the parsley and lemon then stir into the breadcrumbs. Place the halibut onto an ovenproof tray, season with salt and pepper then place on top with the crumb. Bake in a hot oven for 12 minutes, or until the crust is a rich golden brown.

Sauté the kale in a little oil, add the butter and season well.

To serve; Place a good spoonful of beetroot dauphinoise onto your plate, alongside the kale. Top with the baked halibut and serve immediately.

CROQUE-MADAME WITH A MAGPIE TWIST

SERVES 4

8 slices of sour dough bread
400g thinly sliced smoked salmon
500ml whole milk
1 small onion, halved
1 bay leaf
60g butter
60g plain flour
1 teaspoon English mustard

120g Emmental cheese, grated
80g mature cheddar, grated
1 tablespoon parsley, chopped
4 free range eggs
Oil for frying
Freshly ground black pepper
Sprigs of dill to finish

METHOD

Place the milk, bay leaf and onion into a pan and heat slowly to infuse, then strain the milk into a bowl and set aside.

In a separate pan, melt the butter then combine with the flour and mix well. Cook for 1-2 minutes before adding the hot milk, a ladle at a time, whisking until smooth. Once all the milk has been added, simmer for 2-3 minutes before stirring in the Emmental cheese, English mustard and chopped parsley. Season with salt and pepper to taste. Set half of the cheese sauce aside for the topping.

Toast the slices of bread on both sides.

Lay four slices of bread onto a baking sheet. Share the smoked salmon between them and then pour over the cheese sauce.

Top with the other slices of toast. Pour over the remaining cheese sauce and top with the Cheddar cheese. Place the sandwiches under a preheated grill until bubbling and starting to brown a little.

Whilst the sandwiches are under the grill, heat a little oil in a frying pan and fry the eggs.

Remove the sandwiches from the grill and place them onto a serving plate. Top each sandwich with a fried egg and finish with a sprig of dill.

DOVER SOLE AND CRAB PAUPIETTES WITH HOLLANDAISE SAUCE

SERVES 2

4 fillets Dover sole, skinned and boned
300g Whitby crab (use equal amounts of brown and white meat)
2 spring onions, finely chopped
6 crushed peppercorns
1 tablespoon white wine vinegar

2 egg yolks
200g clarified butter
Salt and pepper
300g new potatoes
50g butter
1 tablespoon parsley, chopped

METHOD

Place the new potatoes into boiling salted water and cook until tender. Drain off the water and add the butter and chopped parsley. Using a fork, crush the potatoes and mix through the butter and parsley. Set aside to keep warm.

For the Dover sole; Take one fillet at a time and place in a freezer bag. Use the side of a knife to flatten the fish so that it is of an even thickness. Very lightly season the skinned side. Combine the crab meat with the spring onions and divide the mixture between the four fillets, spreading evenly over each one. Starting from the tail end, roll each fillet up (you can stick a cocktail stick into each one to help keep the shape). Place the Dover sole onto a baking sheet and lightly butter. Bake in a preheated oven (220°C/Gas 8) for about 8 minutes. The fish should feel firm if lightly pressed.

For the hollandaise; First clarify the butter by placing it into a pan and heating gently. Any milk solids will collect on the bottom of the pan and the clarified butter will be above.

Reduce the vinegar with the peppercorns by one third, remove from the heat and add a tablespoon of water. Cool slightly.

Whisk the egg yolks over a bain marie (water bath) to form a sabayon (the egg is cooked when it is the consistency of thick cream). Remove from the heat and cool slightly. Gradually whisk in the warm clarified butter - do this slowly as if you add too much butter at once the sauce might split. If the worst happens don't worry, just whisk in a little warm water. Once all the butter has been added, taste and season with salt.

Serve the Dover sole on crushed potatoes and spoon over the hollandaise sauce. Finish with lemon wedges and fresh herbs.

FIRECRACKER PRAWNS

SERVES 4

600g raw king prawn tails
3 red chillies, finely chopped
1 good handful of fresh coriander, finely chopped
6 spring onions, finely chopped
2-3 cloves of garlic, crushed
2 tablespoon teriyaki sauce
2 tablespoon tomato ketchup
2 tablespoon Sriracha hot sauce
1 tablespoon rice wine vinegar
2 tablespoon light brown sugar
Juice and zest of 2 limes
Half teaspoon ground cumin
1 tablespoon sesame seeds
A little oil for cooking
Jasmine rice and charred pak choi quarters to serve

METHOD

Split the prawns to open them up, but do not cut all the way through. Place in a bowl with the chillies, garlic, teriyaki, ketchup, Sriracha, rice wine vinegar, brown sugar, juice and zest of limes and the cumin. Mix well and leave to marinade for at least a couple of hours or overnight.

Cook the rice to the instructions on the package.

Dry fry the pak choi in a hot heavy-based pan, turning frequently to evenly char before serving.

Once the prawns have absorbed the flavours, remove them but save the marinade. Cook the prawns in a preheated pan with a little oil for 2-3 minutes over a relatively high heat to get a little bit of colour onto them. Add the marinade. Bring to the boil. Cook for another couple of minutes or until the marinade has reduced a little, enough to coat the prawns. Add the sesame seeds and chopped coriander and stir through.

To serve, place the rice into lightly-oiled ramekins or small pudding bowls and turn out in the centre of the plates alongside some charred pak choi, share the prawns between each plate. Finish with plenty of finely-chopped spring onions.

TRADITIONAL WHITBY FISH & CHIPS

SERVES 4

4 fillets of fresh cod or haddock
   (about 180g per fillet or 200g for haddock
   to allow for the skin)
2kg good frying potatoes
Beef dripping for frying
   (rapeseed oil if you prefer)

For the batter
500g plain flour
200g self-raising flour
Half teaspoon baking powder
Approx 1 litre chilled water (you may need
   more or less as flours can absorb differently)

METHOD

Firstly make the batter; Sieve the flour into a bowl with the baking powder, then gradually add the water, whisking continually to avoid any lumps. The batter should be the consistency of single cream – too thick and the batter will be crisp on the outside yet stodgy on the inside. Place in the fridge to chill.

Slowly heat the dripping to approx 150°C in a large pan (the dripping should come no more than halfway up the pan, any more and you run the risk of overflowing).

Peel and cut the potatoes into thick chips (the thicker the better as thicker chips absorb less fat). Rinse and pat dry. Carefully add the chips to the fat and cook until soft but still slightly firm. Remove and cool slightly.

Turn up the heat to 175°C. Taking the fillets of fish one at a time, dip into the batter and gently put them into the hot fat. These should take about 7-8 minutes to cook. The batter should look light, golden and crispy. Remove and place onto kitchen paper to drain.

Next place the chips into the hot fat and cook until crisp and golden. Drain on kitchen paper.

Serve with a big dish of tartare sauce, lemon wedges, salt and vinegar.

GARLIC KING SCALLOP AND SQUID

SERVES 4

12 king scallops
300g fresh squid, cleaned
3 cloves of garlic, crushed
100g butter
1 tablespoon parsley, chopped
Salt and black pepper
Thai basil leaves to finish

METHOD

Split the squid so that it can lay flat and, using the tip of a sharp knife, score the inside of the squid then rotate it 90 degrees and score across to give a criss-cross pattern. Cut into strips approximately 1cm wide and set aside.

Heat a little oil in a pan. Place the king scallops in one by one in a clockwise direction around the pan. Cook over a moderately high heat for about a minute, then starting from the top of the pan in a clockwise direction again, turn each scallop over and cook for a further 45 seconds to a minute. Remove the scallops from the pan and place them onto kitchen paper. Keep warm.

Add a little more oil to the pan and turn up the heat. Once the pan is hot carefully add the squid and cook over a high heat for approximately 1 minute before adding the garlic followed by the butter. Allow the butter to melt and start bubbling before returning the king scallops back to the pan along with the chopped parsley, salt and black pepper.

Divide the scallops and squid equally into bowls, sprinkle over micro Thai basil leaves and serve with freshly-baked bread.

GREEN PEPPER SQUID

SERVES 2

200g fresh cleaned squid (ask your fishmonger to open the tube so it can be cleaned better)
1 medium onion
1 green pepper
1 clove of garlic
2 spring onions
Oil for cooking
Light soy sauce
Black pepper

METHOD

Place the main tube of the squid flat on a chopping board and score the inside in a criss-cross pattern. Be careful not to cut all the way through. Cut the squid into strips. If you have the tentacles, rinse them under cold running water rubbing between your hands to remove the cartilage rings from within the suckers. Dry with paper towel and set aside.

Thinly slice the green pepper and onion. Cut the spring onion into 1-2cm pieces and crush the garlic.

Heat a little oil in a frying pan and once smoking hot, add the peppers and onions. Stir fry for 1 minute then add the garlic and squid. Cook for 2-3 minutes, tossing frequently until the squid turns opaque then add the soy sauce and black pepper. Stir fry for a further minute and then share between two bowls and serve immediately.

HADDOCK WITH GARLIC AND SHALLOT

SERVES 2

2 x 200g portions of haddock
2 bulbs of garlic
6 banana shallots
2 sprigs of thyme for cooking
2 sprigs of thyme, leaves pulled off the stalk
Parsley, chopped

300g baby potatoes
Olive oil
Butter
2 tablespoon grated parmesan
Salt and pepper

METHOD

The garlic and shallot can be cooked up to a week in advance and stored in the oil it was cooked in.

Peel and remove the hard stem off each bulb of garlic and place into an ovenproof dish. Peel the shallots and cut into quarters lengthways and add these to the garlic along with the two sprigs of thyme. Cover the garlic and shallots with olive oil and cover the dish with tin foil and then a tightly fitting lid and place into a preheated oven (100°C/Gas 2) for a minimum of 6 hours or even overnight. Once cooked the garlic should be soft and quite opaque. Remove from the oven and either set aside or if you are making this quite in advance, place it into jars and cover with the olive oil from the ovenproof dish and a tightly-fitting lid.

Boil the potatoes in salted water until tender. Strain off the water and using the same pan, add a little oil. Crush the potatoes a little with the back of a fork. Fry the potatoes until they have turned slightly golden then add the butter. Fold through until melted and then fold through the grated parmesan, salt and pepper to taste.

For the haddock; Heat a little oil in a large frying pan, season the haddock with salt and pepper, then carefully lay the fillet into the pan (flesh side down). Pan fry for 4 minutes over a moderately high heat and then turn the fillets over and cook for another 4 minutes.

Take some of the garlic and shallot in oil and using the side of your spoon, smash the garlic a little. Spoon over the haddock, sprinkle with the thyme leaves and place under a preheated grill for 2 minutes or until the garlic has just started to caramelise.

To serve; Place a good spoonful of the parmesan potatoes onto plates, sit the haddock on top and finally spoon over some garlic and shallot oil, finish with chopped parsley.

HAKE WITH MUSSEL AND POTATO KORMA

SERVES 4

4 x 200g skinless hake
8 slices of prosciutto ham
1 kg fresh mussels
500g cooked baby potatoes, diced
2 heaped tablespoons finely grated ginger
4 cloves of garlic puréed
1 red chilli
3 onions, finely chopped
Oil for cooking
2 tablespoon ground coriander
2 teaspoon turmeric
2 teaspoon garam masala
Good pinch of black pepper
300ml thick plain yoghurt
150g creamed coconut
Water
Salt to taste
4 heaped tablespoon ground almonds
Juice of half a lemon
1 tablespoon chopped coriander

METHOD

For the sauce; Blend the chopped onion, ginger, garlic and chilli to a smooth paste. Add a little water to help if needed.

Heat the oil in a pan and add the coriander, black pepper, turmeric and garam masala and stir-fry over a low heat for 1 minute. Turn up the heat, add the onion paste and stir-fry for 10 minutes. Add the creamed coconut, yoghurt and half a litre of water. Stir to dissolve the coconut then add the ground almonds. Bring to the boil and reduce to a gentle simmer. Cook for 30 minutes.

For the hake; Wrap each piece of fish in two slices of prosciutto, heat a little oil in a pan and carefully lay in each piece of fish. Sear around all of the fish, turning the ham crispy, then transfer to a preheated moderate oven for 8-10 minutes or until the fish feels slightly firm.

Add the fresh mussels and potatoes to the sauce. Cover with a lid and cook until the mussels have fully opened (discard any that do not open). Once cooked, remove the pan from the heat and stir in the lemon juice, coriander and salt to taste.

Serve the hake on the mussel and potato korma with freshly boiled rice and naan bread on the side.

HALIBUT AND WILD MUSHROOM FRICASSÉE

SERVES 4

1kg halibut fillet skin on and cut into 4 pieces
350g fresh wild mushrooms
4 shallots, sliced
Splash of brandy
Dash of mushroom ketchup
150ml chicken stock

300ml double cream
10g fresh tarragon
75g butter
Oil
Salt and pepper
Boiled rice to serve

> If you are using dried mushrooms, soak in warm water for an hour or so before use and rinse thoroughly before cooking them.

METHOD

Heat a little oil in a pan and add the mushrooms and shallots. Sauté until golden in colour then add the brandy and the chicken stock and reduce by half before adding the cream. Over a medium heat, reduce this by a third. Turn down the heat and add the butter. Shake the pan to mix and add the fresh tarragon leaves. Season with salt and pepper. Set aside to keep warm.

For the halibut; Season the fish with salt and pepper and heat a little oil in a frying pan. Add the halibut flesh side down. Cook on a medium/high heat for about 3-5 minutes or until golden. Turn once and cook for a further 5-6 minutes.

Place the halibut onto plates and spoon the fricassée next to the fish. Serve with boiled rice.

HERBY COD BAKE

SERVES 4

4 x 200g cod loins
500g part boiled new potatoes, sliced
Half onion, thinly sliced
3 sprigs parsley
2 sprigs thyme
4 sprigs tarragon
2 sprigs sage
3 sprigs basil

6-8 chives
1 clove of garlic
Zest of half a lemon
1 tablespoon Dijon mustard
200ml olive oil
Salt and pepper
Oil for cooking

METHOD

In a food processor, blitz together the parsley, thyme, tarragon, sage, basil and chives with the Dijon mustard, zest of lemon, clove of garlic and olive oil. When the herbs are well chopped and mixed thoroughly, season with salt and pepper. Pour this marinade into a bowl or dish and add the loins of cod. Thoroughly coat the fish in the marinade, cover and place into the fridge overnight.

The next day, heat a deep ovenproof tray on the stove top and add the sliced potatoes and sliced onion with a little oil. Cook on a fairly high heat to impart a little colour. Remove the fish from the marinade and place onto the potatoes, then transfer the tray onto the top shelf of a preheated oven (220°C/Gas 7). Bake for 15-20 minutes or until the fish is cooked.

Serve straight to the table.

HOT CODS

SERVES 4

8 x 125g cod strips (approx. 10cm in length)
Plain flour
4 eggs
Breadcrumbs

For the mustard cheese sauce
100g mature cheddar
100g emmental
200g mozzarella
2 teaspoon English mustard
2 teaspoon wholegrain mustard
100ml milk
Finely sliced green chillies to finish

For the bbq sauce
1 medium onion, finely diced
1 stick of celery, finely diced
1 clove of garlic, crushed
800g tin chopped tomatoes
2 tablespoon tomato ketchup
Half teaspoon ground ginger
1 teaspoon smoked paprika
Half teaspoon Chinese five spice
1 tablespoon Worcestershire sauce
60g dark brown sugar
75ml white wine vinegar
Salt and pepper
Oil

METHOD

For the bbq sauce; Heat a little oil and add the onion, celery and garlic. Cook for 3-4 minutes until lightly coloured. Add the tomatoes, spices, ketchup and Worcestershire sauce. Bring to the boil and reduce to a simmer.

In a separate pan boil together the vinegar and sugar to a light syrup and add to the tomatoes. Cook for around 25-30 minutes or until thickened slightly. Season to taste.

For the cod; Place some flour onto a plate and season with salt and pepper. Beat the eggs and place into a bowl. Place the breadcrumbs in a third bowl. Take each strip of cod and roll through the flour then the egg and finally the breadcrumbs. Repeat this process with each piece of fish to double coat. Deep fry the cod until golden and crispy (these should take about 4-6 minutes to cook). Drain them on kitchen paper to remove any excess oil and season with a little salt.

For the mustard cheese; Heat the milk in a pan and add the cheeses and mustards. Stir until well mixed and stringy.

To serve; Split eight finger rolls and sit in a cod dog, spoon over some bbq sauce and then some mustard cheese. Top with finely chopped green chillies.

KEDGEREE

SERVES 2

2 x smoked haddock fillets (150g each)
1 small onion, finely chopped
200g basmati rice
150ml milk
100ml double cream
1 teaspoon curry paste
2 eggs

Coriander, chopped
1 knob of butter
Pepper
1 tablespoon oil
Dill to garnish

METHOD

Cook the smoked haddock by poaching in water for 3-4 minutes. Remove from the pan and set aside. Once cool enough to handle, pick and flake the haddock fillets, removing any skin and bones. Set to one side.

For the rice; Heat the oil and add the onion, sauté for a minute and add the curry paste, cook for a further minute. Add the rice and stir in the milk and cream. Bring to the boil and reduce to a very gentle simmer. Place a lid onto the pan and cook for around 10-12 minutes or until the liquid has been absorbed and the rice is cooked. Add a little water if the rice becomes too dry.

Bring some water to the boil and carefully lower in the eggs. Boil for 3 minutes. Remove the eggs from the pan and place into cold water for a minute to cool.

Remove the shells and roughly chop the eggs. Stir through the rice with the butter, coriander, pepper and smoked haddock. Check the seasoning and serve immediately with sprigs of dill.

LOBSTER CARBONARA

SERVES 2

1 whole cooked lobster, dressed
120g dried tagliatelle pasta
100g smoked pancetta
250ml double cream
30g butter
2 banana shallots, thinly sliced
1 clove of garlic, crushed

1 egg yolk
1 tablespoon parsley, chopped
30g grated parmesan cheese
Salt and pepper
Oil for cooking

METHOD

Place the pasta into boiling salted water and cook as per instructions.

Cut the pancetta into small lardons. Place into a pan with a tiny amount of oil, cook until golden in colour then add the sliced shallots and crushed garlic. Sauté for a couple of minutes, add the cream, bring to the boil and then reduce to a simmer.

Whilst the cream is coming to the boil, cut up the lobster meat and add to the cream, simmering to warm through. Add the butter and swirl the pan to mix in.

Remove the pan from the heat, stir in the beaten egg yolk and then the grated parmesan.

Strain the pasta and add to the lobster cream with the chopped parsley and salt and pepper to taste. Toss the pasta and cream thoroughly.

Share between two plates and serve immediately with fresh ciabatta.

LOBSTER AND QUEEN SCALLOP BROTH WITH POTATO DUMPLINGS

SERVES 2

150g queen scallops
100g cooked lobster
150g potato gnocchi
1 carrot, cut into julienne
Quarter stick of celery, cut into julienne
Quarter leek, cut into julienne
1 small fennel, cut into julienne

50ml dry white wine
200ml fish stock
300ml vegetable stock
2 teaspoon parsley, chopped
Salt and pepper

METHOD

For the broth; Place the wine and both stocks into a pan, add the julienne of vegetables. Bring to the boil and reduce to a gentle simmer. Cook for 5 minutes then add the queen scallops and gnocchi, season with salt and pepper and cook for a further 3 minutes (the gnocchi will float to the surface when cooked). Add the cooked lobster and cook for a further 2 minutes to warm through. Finish the broth with the chopped parsley. Transfer into bowls and serve with warm bread.

LOBSTER, MAC 'N' CHEESE

SERVES 4

4 cooked lobsters
300g dried macaroni
4 slices smoked streaky bacon, cut into lardons
50g butter
50g plain flour
650ml whole milk
Half onion studded with 6 cloves
2 bay leaves
2 green chillies, very finely sliced
100g mature Cheddar, grated

100g Gruyère cheese, grated
50g parmesan cheese, grated
100g goats cheese, crumbled
1 teaspoon English mustard
Pinch smoked paprika
Salt and pepper
2 tablespoons Panko breadcrumbs
Oil for cooking
50g butter

METHOD

Cook the macaroni in salted water until al dente, drain and set aside.

Prepare the lobsters. Pull off the tails and remove the shell. Cut the tails in half, lengthways and remove intestinal tract. Set aside four halves and chop up the remainder. Remove the meat from the rest of the lobster by pulling off the legs and crushing them with a rolling pin to extract the meat. Crack the claws and remove the meat (hopefully this may come out still in the shape of the claw. If it does set four aside with the half tails). Pick the remainder of the meat from claw arms and finally split the head, discard the sac and remove any meat from the shell. Add all this to the chopped tail.

For the sauce, gently heat the milk with the studded onion and bay leaves. Remove the milk from the heat just before it boils and set aside for 10 minutes to infuse. Remove the onion and bay leaves. In a deep pan, melt the 50g of butter then add the lardons of bacon and finely-sliced chillies.

Cook for about a minute or until softened then add the plain flour and mix to a paste. Gently cook the roux until it takes on a slightly sandy texture, then gradually start to whisk in the infused milk a ladle at a time, bringing the sauce back to the boil before adding the next ladle. Continue this until all the milk has been used. Next add the mustard and paprika, followed by the Cheddar, Gruyère and parmesan. Taste and add salt and pepper as required. Stir in the macaroni and chopped lobster and place this into an ovenproof dish.

Mix the breadcrumbs and goats cheese together and sprinkle over the top of the pasta. Place the dish into a preheated oven (200°C/Gas 8) for 5-10 minutes or until the topping has toasted.

Whilst the pasta is in the oven heat the other 50g of butter in a pan and lightly saute the pieces of lobster until piping hot.

To serve simply spoon the Mac 'n' Cheese onto plates and top with the sautéed lobster tail and claw. Finish with freshly chopped herbs.

MACKEREL WITH POMEGRANATE AND GOATS CHEESE

SERVES 4 AS A STARTER

4 mackerel, filleted and pin-boned
1 pomegranate
150g goats cheese, crumbled
Handful of watercress
Handful of rocket leaves
50ml olive oil
30ml red wine vinegar
2 slices of white bread
2 tablespoon of oil for cooking
Knob of butter
Salt and pepper

METHOD

First make the croutons; Remove the crusts and cut the bread into small cubes (about ½cm squared). Heat a tablespoon of oil in a pan and stir in the knob of butter. Fry the bread and over a low to medium heat, tossing the pan regularly to cook and evenly colour the croutons. Once they are golden in colour, remove from the heat and place onto kitchen paper to draw excess oil from them. Set aside.

Make the dressing by simply mixing together the olive oil and red wine vinegar with some salt and pepper. Shake vigorously to emulsify.

Cut the pomegranate in half and using a spoon, tap the pomegranate over a bowl to knock out all the seeds. Set aside.

Heat a little oil in a pan and season the mackerel fillets with salt and pepper. Carefully lay each fillet into the hot pan flesh side down, cook for a minute over a moderately high heat and then turn the fillets over and cook for a further 2 minutes. The skin should be quite crisp and the fish should feel firm. Remove the pan from the heat and rest while you dress your plates.

To serve; Mix the watercress, rocket and dressing together. Share the salad between four and sprinkle over the pomegranate seeds, croutons and goats cheese. Place the mackerel fillets, skin side-up, on top of the salad and serve immediately.

MAGPIE FISHCAKES

MAKES 8–12

1½kg potatoes (floury potatoes like Maris Piper or King Edward)
1½kg skinless and boneless white fish (cod, haddock or whiting are good to use)
1 bunch of spring onions, finely chopped
Fish stock (to poach the fish)
2 bay leaves
1 tablespoon sage, chopped

1 tablespoon parsley, chopped
Salt and pepper
Flour for dusting
3 eggs, beaten
White breadcrumbs
Oil for cooking
Lemon wedges to serve

METHOD

Peel and chop the potatoes, place them into a pan of salted water and bring to the boil. Reduce the heat and cook for 15-20 minutes or until the potatoes are soft but not falling apart.

Drain the water from the potatoes and mash until very smooth. Add the chopped parsley, sage and spring onions to the potatoes along with salt and pepper. Set aside to cool.

Place the fish in a separate pan, cover with fish stock and add the bay leaves. Cook over a low heat. Once the fish is cooked, remove the bay leaves and drain off the stock. Add the fish to the potato and mix in well. Taste the mix and add more salt and pepper if required. Leave the mix to completely cool down and firm up before the next step.

Once the fishcake mix has completely cooled divide into 8-12 portions (depending on the size that you require). Roll each into a ball and then flatten them to about 1½cm thick. Tidy and shape each to resemble a wheel then dust each with flour (knocking off any excess). Submerge in the beaten egg, ensuring each fishcake is completely coated then finally roll each through the breadcrumbs, again making sure that all are completely coated. Place the fishcakes into the fridge for 30 minutes to firm up before frying.

Heat a little oil in a pan and carefully lay in each fishcake. Over a moderately low to medium heat, pan fry the fishcakes on each side for 4-6 minutes or until golden in colour and piping hot inside. Serve either with homemade mushy peas or with a salad of crunchy pickles and a citrusy mayonnaise.

MONKFISH AND SAUSAGE CASSEROLE

SERVES 2

400g monkfish fillet, cut into 10 pieces
200g pork mince
2 slices smoked streaky bacon, finely chopped
1 slice white bread, blitzed to a fine crumb
5g fresh sage, chopped
1 teaspoon dried marjoram
1 teaspoon parsley, chopped
150ml red wine

Splash of port
1 x 400g tin rich chopped tomatoes
100ml chicken stock
2 carrots, finely chopped
Half leek, finely chopped
Salt and pepper
Oil for cooking

METHOD

Marinade the monkfish in the red wine for a minimum of 2 hours or overnight before cooking.

To make the sausage; Mix together the pork mince, bacon, breadcrumbs, herbs, port, salt and pepper. Split the mixture into 16 and roll into balls. You will only need half of these so chill or freeze the rest for another time.

Heat a little oil in a pan and add the sausage balls. Over a moderate heat brown the sausage all around. Pour the red wine that the monkfish has been marinating in into the pan and reduce by two-thirds.

Add the stock, carrot and leek. Cook for a minute and then add the tomatoes. Bring to the boil and then reduce to a simmer. Add the monkfish, cover the pan with a lid and cook for 6-8 minutes. Taste the sauce and adjust the seasoning to your liking.

Serve with plenty of herby mashed potatoes.

MUSHY PEAS

SERVES 6

500g dried marrowfat peas
1 rounded teaspoon bicarbonate of soda
1 rounded teaspoon of salt
1 rounded teaspoon of sugar
Half teaspoon of pea green colouring

METHOD

Place the peas into a deep pan and add warm water. Thoroughly wash the peas by using your hand to rub the peas together. The water will change colour so drain off the dirty water and repeat by covering the peas with fresh warm water and rubbing them together. Do this two or three times until the water is pretty clear. Drain then cover the peas with cold water and stir in the bicarbonate of soda until it is fully dissolved. You will need the water to be triple the depth of the peas as they will absorb a lot of this water. Leave the peas to soak overnight.

Repeat the cleaning process, drain off the cloudy water and repeat.

Cover the peas with hot water and place the pan onto the heat. Add the salt, sugar and pea colouring (optional). Bring to the boil and then reduce the heat to a simmer. Cook the peas for between 45 minutes and an hour or until the peas have 'dropped' (lost their shape and gone mushy).

The peas are now ready to serve with Whitby fish and chips.

MUSSELS AND CHIPS

SERVES 4

2kg white potatoes (King Edwards are ideal)
Beef dripping for deep frying
2kg fresh mussels
80g butter
6 shallots, finely sliced
3 cloves of garlic, crushed
300ml Chardonnay
200ml double cream
Parsley, chopped

METHOD

Place the dripping into a deep pan – no more than half way up and heat to 140°C. (note; never leave a pan of fat unattended). Peel the potatoes and cut them into chips, the thicker the better as they will absorb less fat the thicker they are. Blanch the chips in the dripping until firm but soft in the middle, remove and set aside. Heat the dripping to around 180°C ready to finish the chips.

For the mussels; Firstly pull away any beard (this is the woolly/hairy bit that is attached to the side of the mussel) and rinse under cold running water. Discard any that do not close. Heat the butter in a pan and add the shallot and garlic. Over a moderate heat, sauté these without adding any colour but until soft and opaque. Increase the heat and add the Chardonnay.

Cover with a tightly fitting lid and steam for 4-5 minutes or until they have all opened, discarding any that do not open. Share the mussels between four bowls, reserving the cooking liquor. Place the pan of liquor back onto the heat and bring to the boil. Add the cream, bring back to the boil and reduce by a third.

Finish the chips by carefully putting them back into the hot dripping. Fry until crisp and golden. Remove the chips from the pan and drain onto kitchen paper. Lightly season. Place into a large bowl to share.

The mussel liquor should now have reduced by a third. Sprinkle on the chopped parsley and then pour over the mussels and serve immediately with the chips and some garlic mayonnaise.

OAK ROAST SALMON FISHCAKES

SERVES 4

500g oak roast salmon
250g fresh salmon fillet
800g peeled potatoes
   (King Edwards or Maris Pipers)
2 egg yolks
8 spring onions, finely sliced
Juice and zest of half a lemon
1 tablespoon chives, chopped
1 tablespoon parsley, chopped
Salt and pepper

For the pané
Plain flour
4 eggs
10 slices white bread, made into breadcrumbs
Dripping or rapeseed oil for deep frying

METHOD

Cook the potatoes in boiling salted water until tender, drain off the water then mash, seasoning with salt and black pepper. Add both egg yolks, sliced spring onions, juice and zest of the lemon, chopped chives and the chopped parsley. Set aside.

Poach the fresh salmon in water, salt and pepper. Once the fish is cooked, drain off the water and flake the fish into the potato along with the oak roast salmon. Vigorously mix to evenly spread the fish. Leave to cool slightly.

When cooled enough to handle, divide the mix into 8-12 portions. Roll into balls then flatten slightly to resemble a wheel.

For the pané; Put some plain flour onto a plate and season with salt and pepper. In a bowl whisk the eggs. Place the breadcrumbs into a different bowl. One at a time, lightly flour each fishcake, then roll through the egg and finally through the breadcrumbs. Repeat this with all of them and chill, while you heat the dripping.

Use a deep pan for deep frying and fill no more than half full. Heat the dripping/oil to 175°C and gently lay in the fishcakes (I would recommend cooking four at a time. They should take approx 4-5 minutes or until golden brown. Remove from the pan and place onto kitchen paper to drain.

Serve on dressed leaves with Horseradish cream.

ONE POT HAKE

SERVES 4

4 x 200g hake fillets, cut into bite-size pieces
200g cooked ham hock, roughly chopped
100g smoked bacon, cut into lardons
2 leeks, washed and sliced
2 cloves of garlic, finely sliced
1 stick of celery, finely sliced
4 carrots, diced
800g baby potatoes, sliced

500ml fish stock
500ml chicken stock
50g butter
2 tablespoon oil
Parsley, chopped
Salt and pepper

METHOD

Heat the oil in a large pan and add the smoked bacon lardons. Sauté the lardons until crisp. Add the ham hock, leeks, garlic and celery. Sauté for a further couple of minutes and add the sliced potatoes and both stocks. Bring to the boil. Transfer to an ovenproof dish, place a lid on and put into a preheated oven (200°C/Gas 8) for 30 minutes.

Remove from the oven and season the hake. Take the lid off the pan and add the butter. Stir through and return to the oven without the lid. Cook for a further 20 minutes.

Carefully remove the dish from the oven and gently stir through the chopped parsley and salt and pepper.

Serve immediately with lots of freshly baked bread.

OYSTERS WITH TOMATO AND CAPER

SERVES 4

24 rock oysters
3 shallots, very finely diced
6 tomatoes, skinned and deseeded
1 tablespoon capers
Splash of white wine
75g butter
1 tablespoon chervil, chopped
1 tablespoon oil
Black pepper

METHOD

Remove the oysters from their shells, retaining the deep half of the shell.

Heat the oil in a pan and add the finely chopped shallots. Sauté over a low heat until softened. Add the oysters and turn up the heat. Reduce any juices then add the splash of wine, tomatoes and capers. Reduce the liquor a little more before adding the butter. Remove the pan from the heat and stir in the chervil and freshly-milled black pepper.

Sit the oysters back into their shells and spoon over the caper and tomato dressing.

PAN FRIED MACKEREL, PARMA HAM AND ASPARAGUS

SERVES 4

4 mackerel, filleted
12-16 asparagus spears, trimmed and blanched
8 slices Parma ham
4 pickled onions, finely sliced
Oil for cooking
Salt and pepper

For the vinaigrette
1 tablespoon wholegrain mustard
3 tablespoon red wine vinegar
9 tablespoon extra virgin olive oil
1 tablespoon honey
Salt and black pepper
Fresh herbs to garnish

METHOD

For the vinaigrette; Place the mustard, vinegar, olive oil and honey into a bowl and whisk until well combined. Season with salt and freshly milled black pepper.

For the mackerel; Remove any bones (these run down the centre of the fillet) with a pair of tweezers. Season each fillet with a little salt and pepper.

Heat a little oil in a pan and carefully lay in each fillet of mackerel, skin side down. Cook over a moderately high heat for 2-3 minutes or until the skin is crispy. Turn the fillets of mackerel over and continue to cook for a further 2 minutes.

In a separate pan heat a little oil and add the spears of asparagus. Season with salt and pepper and over a high heat char the spears, tossing frequently.

To assemble the dish, plate the asparagus spears then add folds of Parma ham followed by rings of pickled onions and then the mackerel fillets. Top with fresh herbs and finally drizzle over the mustard dressing and serve.

PAN FRIED SKATE WING WITH WARM PICKLE SALAD

SERVES 2

2 x 350g skate wings
Flour for dusting
Salt and pepper
6 gherkins
2 pickled onions
4 balsamic onions
1 tablespoon capers
200g new potatoes
2 spring onions
Mixed salad leaves
Olive oil

METHOD

Place the potatoes into boiling salted water and cook until tender. Drain and keep warm.

Season some plain flour with salt and pepper. Dust the skate wings with the flour, knocking off any excess.

Heat a little oil in a frying pan and carefully lay in the fish (thickest side first). Pan-fry for around 5 minutes or until golden in colour then turn the fish over and cook for a further 4-5 minutes. Once cooked, remove from the pan and sit on kitchen paper.

Whilst the skate is cooking, thinly slice the gherkins, pickled onions and spring onions. Cut the balsamic onions in half. Add these to the cooked potatoes, drizzle over a little olive oil and season with salt and pepper, toss until well mixed. Add the mixed leaves to the potatoes along with the capers. Toss to mix.

To serve, place the skate wing onto the plate and spoon on a generous portion of the warm pickle salad and serve.

PIRI PIRI MACKEREL

SERVES 4

For the piri piri marinade
4 whole mackerel, gutted and cleaned
6 hot red chillies (like scotch bonnet), roughly chopped
2 teaspoon sweet smoked paprika
6 cloves of garlic, roughly chopped
1 teaspoon oregano
2 tablespoon red wine vinegar
Juice and zest of 1 lemon
100ml olive oil
Salt and black pepper

For the tomato and scallion rice
500g cooked rice
1 bunch spring onions, chopped
2 teaspoon sweet smoked paprika
4 tablespoon tomato purée
12 cherry tomatoes, quartered
1 tablespoon parsley, chopped
Oil for cooking

METHOD

For the marinade; Place the chillies, smoked paprika, garlic, oregano, vinegar and oil in a food processor. Blitz until well combined then add the juice and zest of the lemon and season with plenty of salt and pepper. Pour this into a jar and store in the fridge for up to a month.

Wash the mackerel, score one side of each and place them onto a baking sheet. Generously brush the fish with the piri piri marinade and place into a preheated oven (200°C/Gas 7) for 12-18 minutes or until cooked through.

For the rice; Heat a little oil and add the cooked rice, tomato purée and a couple of tablespoons of water. Stir continuously for a couple of minutes before adding the spring onions and tomatoes. Mix well and continue to heat through for a further couple of minutes or until piping hot. Remove the rice from the heat and stir in the chopped parsley. Season with salt and pepper.

To serve; Spoon the rice onto plates and sit on the piri piri mackerel. Pour over any juices from the fish and serve immediately with mixed leaves.

PRAWN, MUSSEL AND CRAB SPANISH TORTILLA

SERVES 4

8 king prawn tails, split in half lengthways
200g mussel meat
200g Whitby crab meat
50g anchovy fillets, finely chopped
250g sliced cooked potato
1 medium onion, very finely sliced
1 sweet red pepper, very finely sliced

8 eggs
50ml double cream
1 tablespoon tarragon, chopped
2 spring onions, finely chopped
Pepper
Oil

METHOD

Beat the eggs, add the cream and anchovies. Season with pepper.

Heat a little oil in a 10-inch frying pan (non-stick if you have one) and cook the sliced onion and red pepper. Fry until tender and coloured slightly. Add the prawns and cook for 2 minutes then stir in the potatoes, mussels, crab and spring onions. Mix well then pour in the egg mixture. Cook over a medium heat using use a pallet knife to ensure the it does not stick to the sides. Once the egg has started to set and is losing its wobble, place a plate over the top of the pan and turn out the tortilla and slide it back into the pan (if you're feeling brave) to cook and colour the other side. Alternatively place the pan under a hot grill or into a hot oven to finish the cooking process.

Serve the tortilla on plate with salad leaves and aioli (to make your own, soak a few strands of saffron in a teaspoon of hot water. In a food processor, blitz two cloves of garlic with two egg yolks and a teaspoon of Dijon mustard to a paste. Add the saffron then slowly pour in oil – around 300ml – whilst blending to form a thick mayonnaise sauce).

ROAST COD WITH LANGOUSTINES, BORLOTTI BEANS AND HAM

SERVES 4

4 x 200g cod fillets, skin on
1 medium onion, finely diced
2 medium carrots, finely diced
1 fennel, finely diced
1 clove of garlic, crushed
400g cooked borlotti beans
1 cooked ham hock, stripped
Vegetable stock or the liquor from the hock
50g unsalted butter, cut into cubes
Parsley, chopped
Salt and pepper

For the garnish
8 langoustine tails, shelled and deveined
100g self-raising flour
1 teaspoon cornflour
Chilled sparkling water
Pinch of salt
Oil for deep frying (rapeseed or sunflower)
4 spring onions
Lemon and pea shoots for serving

(See page 26 for cooking your own ham hock)

METHOD

In a pan, heat a little oil and gently cook the onion, carrot and fennel. Lightly sauté without colour and add the garlic and borlotti beans. Cover the beans with stock or the liquor from the hock and bring to the boil. Reduce to a simmer. Cook gently to reduce the stock by a third then add the ham hock to warm through. Finish the beans with the butter by dropping in a little at a time and swirling the pan to combine it. Add the parsley and season as required.

Heat a little oil in a pan, season the cod with salt and pepper. Carefully place the fish in the pan, skin side down and cook over a moderate/high heat for 2-3 minutes. Turn the fish over and cook for a further 2 minutes before placing into a preheated oven (220°C/Gas 8,) for 6-8 minutes.

Whilst the fish is cooking, make a batter. Place the flour, cornflour and pinch of salt in a bowl and slowly whisk in the sparkling water until it has the consistency of single cream.

In a deep pan, pour in the oil – fill to about one third. Gently heat the oil. To test when the oil is hot enough to fry, drop a little batter into the oil and it should come straight back to the surface bubbling. Dip the langoustine tails into the batter and carefully lay them into the oil, followed by the spring onions. Deep fry for 2 minutes or until the batter is crisp and golden, turning if necessary. Remove from the oil and place onto kitchen paper to drain.

To serve; Spoon the beans onto warm plates, place the cod onto the beans and top with the langoustines and spring onions. Finish with wedges of lemon and pea shoots.

ROAST MONKFISH WITH CREAMED BRUSSELS GRATIN

SERVES 2

1 whole monkfish tail 5-600g, bone removed and trimmed (you will end up with two pieces which are similar in size and shape)
Small bunch of parsley, chopped
4 cloves of garlic, crushed
Zest of half a lemon
250g brussel sprouts
150g smoked bacon, cut into lardons
1 small onion, sliced

100g cooked chestnuts
200ml double cream
500ml light chicken stock
100g manchego cheese, grated
Fresh breadcrumbs
Salt and pepper
Oil for cooking

METHOD

For the monkfish; In a bowl, mix the parsley, garlic and lemon zest with a little oil, salt and pepper. Spread this paste onto the flatter side of the fish, then bring them together so that the paste is in the centre. Tie with string to hold whilst cooking. Heat a little oil in a pan and cook the fish over a high heat. Seal the fish all the way around then place into a preheated oven (210°C/Gas 7) for 12-14 minutes.

Whilst the Monkfish is cooking, prepare the sprouts. Bring the chicken stock up to the boil, add the sprouts to the pan and cook for around 5 minutes. In a separate pan, heat a little oil and add the bacon lardons. Cook over a medium heat for around 2 minutes before adding the sliced onion.

Strain the sprouts and add these to the bacon and onion. Sauté for a couple of minutes then add the double cream and chestnuts. Bring to the boil and cook for a further 2 minutes before grating in the manchego and seasoning with black pepper.

Transfer the sprouts to an ovenproof dish, sprinkle over the breadcrumbs and place into the oven for a few minutes or until the breadcrumbs have toasted slightly. Remove the monkfish from the oven and leave to rest for 2 minutes.

To serve; Slice the monkfish and place on top of the brussel sprout gratin and serve immediately.

SALMON KIEV 'BON-BONS'

MAKES 12

For the bon-bons
250g skinned salmon
100g white fish (cod or whiting)
150g cream cheese
2 cloves of garlic
1 tablespoon parsley, chopped
Salt and pepper
Plain flour for dusting
2 eggs, beaten
Breadcrumbs for coating

For the tomato and fennel dip
8 ripe tomatoes, quartered
1 bulb of fennel
1 clove of garlic
2 shallots
2 tablespoon of tomato purée
1 tablespoon white vinegar
100ml vegetable stock
Salt and pepper
Rapeseed oil for deep frying

METHOD

For the sauce; Roughly chop the shallots, garlic and fennel and place into a pan with a little oil. Cook until softened without colouring. Add the tomatoes, tomato purée, vinegar and stock. Bring to the boil and cook for around 20 minutes. Remove the pan from the heat and blitz using a stick blender, keeping a little coarse. Season with salt and pepper to taste and set aside on the stove top to keep warm.

For the bon-bons; Mix the cream cheese, garlic and chopped parsley together, then divide the mix into 12 small balls and place them into the freezer to firm up.

Blitz the salmon and cod in a food processor until smooth and season with salt and pepper. Place the mix into the fridge to rest for at least 30 minutes.

Once rested, remove the cream cheese balls from the freezer and cover each with the salmon mixture. Form each into equally-sized balls.

Proceed to coat the salmon with first a dusting of flour, then the egg and finally the breadcrumbs.

Heat the oil for deep frying to 180°C. Carefully insert the bon-bons, deep fry for 3-4 minutes or until golden brown. Remove from the oil and drain on kitchen paper. Serve with plenty of the tomato and fennel dip.

SCALLOPS WITH CAULIFLOWER, ARTICHOKE & CAPERS

SERVES 4

12 king scallops
1 medium cauliflower
Knob of butter
Salt and pepper
Vegetable stock
4 artichoke hearts (cooked ones in oil are ideal)
Oil for cooking

For the final addition
100g butter
1 tablespoon of capers
1 clove of garlic, crushed
Parsley, chopped

METHOD

Cut the cauliflower into small pieces and place into a pan with the knob of butter and just cover with vegetable stock. Bring to the boil and cook for approx 15 minutes or until the cauliflower is tender and there is almost no liquid left in the pan. Blitz to a smooth purée, season to taste.

Cut the artichokes into quarters. In a frying pan, heat a little oil and add the scallops and artichokes, starting from the top of the pan, working clockwise. After 1 minute turn the scallops and artichokes over and cook for a further 1 minute. Add the butter, garlic, capers and parsley. Shake the pan to melt the butter and warm through the garlic and capers whilst also coating the scallops.

To serve; Spoon some cauliflower purée onto the plates, place three scallops and four pieces of artichoke per portion onto the cauliflower, pour over the caper garlic butter and serve.

SCALLOPS WITH BELUGA LENTILS

SERVES 4

12 king scallops
150g dried beluga lentils
1 carrot
Half onion
Half stick of celery
1 clove of garlic
250ml chicken stock
Oil for cooking
50g butter
200ml crème fraiche

METHOD

Soak the beluga lentils in cold water for about an hour to rehydrate. Next, drain the lentils and rinse thoroughly with clean water. Once the water runs clear, set aside.

Carefully chop up the vegetables so that they are very fine. Heat a little oil in a pan and add the vegetables, sauté over a medium heat until softened slightly then add the lentils and chicken stock. Bring the lentils to the boil then reduce the heat to a moderate simmer. Cook for around 25 minutes or until the lentils are soft and tender by which time they will have absorbed most of the stock. Taste and add salt and pepper if necessary. Stir in the butter, set aside.

For the scallops; Heat a little oil in a frying pan and carefully lay in each scallop clockwise around the pan, over a high heat cook for 2 minutes. Turn the scallops over and cook for a further 1-2 minutes.

To serve, place a good spoonful of lentils onto your plates and sit three scallops per portion on top. Finish with a spoonful of crème fraiche and sprinkle with fresh herbs.

SCALLOPS WITH BLACK PUDDING HASH AND BEURRE BLANC

SERVES 4

12 king scallops
200g black pudding
8 baby potatoes
Half onion
1 clove of garlic
50ml olive oil
Parsley, chopped

For the beurre blanc
200ml white wine
100ml white wine vinegar
1 shallot, finely chopped
400g butter, diced

METHOD

Cut the potatoes into small pieces. Dice the black pudding and onion and slice the garlic. Heat the oil in a heavy-based pan and add the potatoes, cook over a moderate heat for 5 minutes, tossing occasionally. Add the black pudding, onion and garlic, mix well and place the pan into a preheated oven (210°C/Gas 7) for around 6-8 minutes. Stir through the chopped parsley.

For the beurre blanc; In a pan mix together the wine, vinegar and shallot and reduce over a moderate heat by two-thirds. Add the butter one piece at a time continually whisking until you have a couple of pieces left then remove the pan from the heat. Whisk in the final couple of pieces of butter off the heat and the sauce should thicken. Set aside.

For the scallops, preheat a pan, add a little oil and then starting from the top side of the pan, place in the scallops one by one. Cook over a moderately high heat for 2 minutes then turn over and cook for a further 1 minute.

To serve, place a good spoonful of the black pudding hash onto each plate, sit on the scallops and then pour over the beurre blanc, Finish with fresh herbs.

SEA BASS WITH PICCALILLI AND ANCHOVIES

SERVES 2

2 x 200g sea bass fillets
8 anchovy fillets
1 tablespoon parsley, chopped
50g butter
Oil for cooking

For the piccalilli
500g cauliflower florets
500g chopped onion, cut into half inch dice
200g deseeded cucumber, cut into half inch dice
200g French beans, halved

350g salt
700ml white malt vinegar
200ml water
3 tablespoon sugar
2 tablespoon English mustard
3 teaspoon ground turmeric
3 teaspoon coriander seeds
1 teaspoon ground ginger
2 cloves of garlic, crushed
2 tablespoon cornflour

METHOD

Place all the vegetables in a bowl and sprinkle over the salt. Mix well, cover with cling film and leave in a cool place for a minimum of 12 hours. The next day, drain off any excess liquid and then rinse the vegetables with plenty of cold running water.

In a pan bring to the boil the vinegar, water, sugar, mustard and the spices. Add the vegetables and simmer for around 10-12 minutes or until the vegetables are quite tender with a slight crunch.

Mix a little water into the cornflour to make a slack paste and then stir this into the vegetables. Simmer for a further 2 minutes and remove from the heat. The liquor should generously coat the back of a spoon.

Spoon the piccalilli into sterilised jars, place on the lid and store in a cool, dark place for a minimum of 2 months.

For the fish; Pan-fry the sea bass fillets in a little oil, flesh side down for 3 minutes. Turn over, add the butter and cook for a further 3-4 minutes basting with the butter. Add the anchovies and chopped parsley to the pan to warm through.

To serve; Place the sea bass fillets onto plates pour over the anchovy butter and serve with a good spoon of piccalilli.

> Piccalilli has to be made at least 2 months in advance for the flavours to develop. If you can't wait buy a good one from your local deli.

SEAFOOD JAMBALAYA

SERVES 4

1 tablespoon oil
1 red onion, thinly sliced
2 rashers of bacon
100g chorizo, cut into small dice
1 red pepper, cut into slices
1 green pepper, cut into slices
2 chillies, finely chopped (seeds left in if you prefer the dish to be hot)
2 cloves of garlic, crushed
2 teaspoons of Cajun spice (if you would prefer to make your own cajun spice you will need equal parts of ground coriander, oregano and ground black pepper to double equal parts smoked paprika and crushed chillies)

400g long grain rice, rinsed
200ml dry white wine
2 tomatoes, peeled and diced
650ml chicken or vegetable stock
Half teaspoon of saffron, soaked in a drop of warm water
16 king prawn tails, peeled and deveined
20 mussels
160g prepared squid, cleaned and scored
100g salmon
100g smoked salmon, cut into strips

METHOD

Heat the oil in a saucepan and gently fry the onion, peppers, bacon and chorizo. Cook for a few minutes until lightly browned, then add the chilli, garlic and Cajun spice. Cook for a couple of minutes.

Stir in the rice to coat with the spices, then pour in the wine. After about a minute stir in the tomato, stock and saffron (including the soaking liquid). Bring to the boil, then reduce to a simmer, cover with a lid and cook for about 10-12 minutes.

Add the prawns, salmon and mussels, replace the lid and cook for 6-8 minutes then add the squid and smoked salmon and cook for a further 3 minutes until the seafood is cooked and the rice is tender.

Serve immediately.

SEAFOOD PAELLA

SERVES 4

600g Callasparra paella rice
1 onion, finely diced
1 red pepper, diced
1 green pepper, diced
2 cloves of garlic, crushed
1 teaspoon paprika
4 chicken thighs, boned and diced
100g pancetta, diced
100g chorizo, diced
250ml white wine
Pinch of saffron (add to the wine 30 minutes prior to using)
1 litre chicken stock

10 cherry tomatoes, halved
200g salmon, chopped into 8 pieces
200g halibut, chopped into 8 pieces
8 king scallops
300g squid, cut into strips
8 king prawns
8 crevettes
16 live mussels, washed, beards removed
12 live clams, washed
100g marsh samphire
Parsley, chopped
3 tablespoon oil
Salt and pepper

METHOD

Heat the oil in a pan (paella pan or heavy-based saute pan). Fry together the chicken, pancetta and chorizo. Cook until well browned. Add the onion, garlic and pepper. Once softened, add the rice. Stir well before adding wine, paprika and cherry tomatoes. Bring to the boil. Cover with the stock, bring back to the boil and lay on the salmon, halibut, prawns and crevettes. Cover the pan with a lid or foil and reduce the heat. Cook for 8 minutes.

Remove the lid, add the scallops, squid, clams and samphire. Taste and season with salt and pepper. Replace the lid and cook for 4-6 minutes or until all the mussels and clams have opened. Remove the pan from the heat, sprinkle with chopped parsley. Serve immediately.

> Chef's Tip; Score the inner side of the squid in a crisscross so when it cooks it curls and has a lovely diamond pattern.

SEAFOOD SPAGHETTI

SERVES 4

500g spaghetti al nero de seppia (squid ink spaghetti)
150ml white wine
Pinch of saffron
50g butter
4 shallots, finely sliced
2 cloves of garlic, crushed
4 tomatoes, skinned, deseeded and roughly chopped

500g fresh mussels
200g clams
200g squid
8 king prawns, cut in half lengthways
1 tablespoon coriander, chopped
2 tablespoon crème fraiche
Squeeze of lemon juice
Oil for cooking
Salt and pepper

METHOD

Place the saffron into the wine at least an hour before using, to infuse.

Cook the spaghetti as per instructions on the packet in salted water.

Wash and de-beard the mussels, score the squid in a criss-cross pattern.

Heat a little oil in a pan and fry the garlic and shallots over a gentle heat. Cook until softened. Turn up the heat and add the mussels and saffron-infused wine, Cover with a tightly-fitting lid and cook for 4 minutes, shaking the pan occasionally.

Remove the mussels from the pan and retain the cooking liquor. When cool enough to handle, pick half the mussels from their shells and set aside.

Add a little oil into the pan and heat. Add the prawns, clams and squid. Over a high heat sauté until the clams have opened, the prawns are pink and the squid has curled. Add the cooking liquor back into the pan along with the butter, chopped tomatoes and coriander, bring to the boil and add the cooked pasta and mussels. Toss the pan to mix together and heat up. Once the juices are boiling again, turn off the heat and add the crème fraiche and squeeze of lemon juice, salt and pepper and mix to coat the pasta and shellfish.

Place the pasta into dishes and serve immediately with freshly baked ciabatta.

SHELLFISH AND SAMPHIRE STIR FRY

SERVES 4

8 crevettes, tails split
200g mussels
150g clams
150g queen scallops
2 tablespoon groundnut oil
8 spring onions, diagonally sliced
2 lemongrass, finely sliced
Half a thumb of ginger, cut into julienne

2 cloves of garlic, finely sliced
300g fresh samphire, woody stems removed
3 tablespoon Shaoxing rice wine
3 tablespoon soy sauce
1 tablespoon sesame seeds
Toasted sesame oil for drizzling

METHOD

Heat a wok and add the groundnut oil. Once the oil is smoking, add the spring onions, lemongrass, ginger and garlic. Cook over a high heat for a minute, tossing the wok and moving the vegetables continuously.

Remove the vegetables from the pan and again over a high heat fry the crevettes, mussels, clams and scallops. Cook the shellfish for 3-4 minutes or until the crevettes have turned orange and the mussels and clams have fully opened.

Add the Shaoxing rice wine, soy sauce and samphire whilst tossing the wok continuously to mix well.

Reduce the cooking liquors down a touch before returning into the pan with the vegetables and the sesame seeds. Stir through.

Divide the stir-fried shellfish into bowls and finish each off with a good drizzle of toasted sesame oil and serve.

SMOKED HADDOCK RAREBIT WITH CONFIT TOMATOES

SERVES 4

4 x 200g smoked haddock fillets
8 slices of ciabatta
Olive oil

For the tomatoes
200g ripe baby plum tomatoes
1 sprig of thyme
2 cloves of garlic
1 bay leaf
1 shallot, finely sliced
Olive oil

For the rarebit
40g butter
40g plain flour
400ml milk
200g mature Cheddar cheese
2 teaspoon Worcestershire sauce
2 teaspoon wholegrain mustard
1 egg yolk
Salt and pepper

METHOD

In a pan, place the tomatoes with the oil, garlic, shallot, thyme and bay leaf. If needed add a little more olive oil to just cover the tomatoes and over a low heat warm to combine the flavours. Infuse on the heat for 30 minutes. Remove from the heat and keep warm.

Heat a little oil in a frying pan and add the smoked haddock. Season with pepper and gently pan fry for 5-6 minutes.

For the sauce; Melt the butter in a pan, stir in the flour. Beat to a paste and cook until it turns a sandy texture. Over a moderately high heat, gradually add the milk, a little at a time, whisking until smooth and returning to the boil each time before adding any more milk. Once all the milk has been incorporated, return to the boil and simmer for 2-3 minutes. Stir in the cheese, mustard and Worcestershire sauce, season with salt and pepper. Remove from the heat and let stand for a couple of minutes. Beat in the egg yolk.

Toast the ciabatta slices on a griddle pan and drizzle with a little olive oil.

Remove the haddock from the pan and place onto a tray. Pour over the rarebit sauce and flash under a preheated grill to brown. Once browned, place the haddock rarebits onto plates and serve with a good spoonful of confit tomatoes and a couple of slices of the ciabatta.

SMOKED SALMON 'SUR LE PLAT'

SERVES 2

400g sliced smoked salmon
1 x 400g tin rich chopped tomatoes
1 small carrot, very finely chopped
1 small onion, very finely chopped
1 clove of garlic, crushed
Quarter stick of celery, finely chopped
2 free range hens eggs
Oil
Salt and pepper

METHOD

Heat a little oil in a saucepan and cook the carrot, onion, celery and garlic. Sauté for a couple of minutes until the vegetables have softened and then add the chopped tomatoes. Simmer for 10 minutes. Put the pieces of haddock into the sauce and gently cook for a couple of minutes. Remove the pan from the heat.

Place the haddock pieces into two separate dishes, lay over the smoked salmon and then pour over the sauce. Place the dishes onto an ovenproof tray and then crack open each egg and place on top of the fish and sauce. Carefully place the dishes into a preheated oven and bake for around 8 minutes or until the egg has set but the yolk is still runny.

Serve with dressed leaves.

SMOKED SALMON SOUFFLÉ

SERVES 6

75g butter
100g plain flour
560ml full fat milk
4 egg yolks
4 egg whites
150g Emmental cheese
50g parmesan cheese
300g smoked salmon

Pinch of cayenne pepper
Pinch of nutmeg
Salt and pepper
200ml crème fraiche
1 tablespoon heather honey
1 tablespoon chopped dill

METHOD

Mix the crème fraiche, honey and dill together and set aside.

Melt the butter in a pan and add the flour. Mix to a paste and continue to cook until it takes on a sandy texture. Gradually add the milk, stirring vigorously and return to the boil each time before adding more milk. Continue this until all the milk has been used. Remove the pan from the heat and beat in the egg yolks and cheese, season with the pinch of cayenne, nutmeg, salt and pepper. Roughly chop 200g of the smoked salmon and mix in. Set aside. Reserve the other 100g of smoked salmon for serving.

Whisk the egg whites until firm.

Prepare the ramekin dishes by brushing the inside with melted butter. Pour out any excess and then add a little plain flour. Shake the flour around the mould to completely coat the inside of it, shaking off any excess.

Fold a third of the egg whites into the salmon mix to loosen the mixture, and then carefully fold in the remainder of the egg white until evenly mixed. Pour into the moulds about two-thirds full.

Place the moulds into a bain-marie (water bath) and carefully place in a preheated oven (200°C/Gas 6) for 25 minutes or until risen and browned.

Remove them from the oven, place onto plates and serve immediately with the remainder of the smoked salmon and salad leaves dressed with honey and dill crème fraiche.

SOLE VERONIQUE

SERVES 4

4 x 200g fillets of Dover or lemon sole (witch or dab are a good cheaper alternative for this dish)
2 shallots, very finely chopped
75ml fish stock
75ml white wine
Butter for lining
Salt and pepper
Handful of seedless green grapes
2 egg yolks

For the fish veloute
30g butter
30g plain flour
300ml fish stock

METHOD

First of all make the fish veloute; In a pan, melt the butter then add the flour and mix well to make a roux (a thick paste). Cook the roux for about 20-30 seconds until it starts to look a little sandy in texture. Gradually add the 300ml of fish stock, whisking all the time to avoid any lumps. Once all the stock has been added, bring the sauce to the boil, reduce the heat and continue to cook for a few minutes more. Remove from the heat and set aside to keep warm.

For the sole; Take a large ovenproof dish and rub the butter generously on the inside, lay in the sole fillets and season with salt and pepper. Add the shallots, 75ml of fish stock and 75ml of white wine. Cover the dish with a tightly-fitting lid or foil and place in a preheated (200°C/Gas 6) oven for 8-12 minutes.

Remove the dish from the oven and strain the cooking liquor into a saucepan. Reduce by half, whisk in the fish veloute and heat. Remove from the heat allow to cool for a minute, then whisk in the egg yolks. Add the grapes into the dish with the sole and carefully pour over the fish sauce.

Place the dish under a preheated grill to lightly brown the sauce, serve with buttered new potatoes.

SOUTHERN FRIED OYSTERS

SERVES 4

24 oysters, shucked
200ml buttermilk
Good splash of tabasco sauce
240g plain flour
200g fine polenta
1-2 tablespoon creole seasoning (you can buy this, but to make your own, combine: 2 tablespoons onion powder, 2 tablespoons garlic powder, 2 tablespoons dried oregano, 2 tablespoons dried basil, 1 tablespoon dried thyme, 1 tablespoon white pepper, 1 tablespoon cayenne pepper, 4 tablespoons paprika, 2 tablespoons salt, 1 teaspoon mustard powder)
Sunflower oil for cooking

For the salsa dip
6 large ripe tomatoes, quartered
1 red chilli, very finely diced
1 small onion, very finely diced
Juice and zest of 1 lime
1 tablespoon coriander, chopped
Pinch of sugar
Salt and pepper to taste
Soured cream
Chopped chives

METHOD

For the salsa, place the tomatoes into a bowl and using a potato masher, mash to a coarse pulp. Add in the chilli, onion, juice and zest of the lime, coriander, sugar, salt and pepper. Mix well and correct the seasoning if required. Cover and place into the fridge.

Mix the soured cream and chives together, cover and place into the fridge.

Place the oysters into a bowl and pour over the buttermilk, Gently fold through the oysters, avoiding damaging them. Cover the oysters and place them into the fridge for a couple of hours. Sift together the plain flour with the polenta. Add the creole seasoning and mix in well, taste the flour mix and add more seasoning if required.

Heat the oil in a deep pan (not more than half full) to 175°C. (never leave a pan of oil unattended). Remove the oysters from the fridge and roll each one through the seasoned flour then transfer to the pan of oil; I would recommend doing this in small batches as they will only take 2-3 minutes to cook. Once the oysters are crispy, remove them from the oil and place on kitchen paper to drain.

To serve, place the oysters back into their shell and serve with the salsa and soured cream dips.

TEMPURA OYSTERS WITH PANCETTA AND A WARM SHERRY DRESSING

SERVES 4

24 oysters
200ml chilled sparkling water
100g plain flour
50g cornflour
2 egg yolks
Half teaspoon salt
Half teaspoon baking powder
Oil for frying
150g pancetta, cut into small dice
24 little gem leaves

For the dressing
1 shallot, finely diced
150ml sweet sherry
1 teaspoon dark brown sugar

METHOD

For the batter; Sieve the flours, baking powder and salt into a bowl and whisk in the egg yolks and the chilled sparkling water until smooth and the consistency of double cream.

Open the oysters and remove them from the shell. Dip into the batter and gently place into hot oil to deep-fry. Cook for approx 2 minutes or until the batter is crisp. Set aside to keep warm.

Sauté the diced pancetta until browned and crispy then remove from the pan. Add the shallot and cook for 30 seconds then finish with the sherry and dark brown sugar. Bring to the boil to dissolve the sugar and thicken slightly, remove from the heat and place into a jug.

To serve; Place an oyster into each little gem leaf, add a few pieces of pancetta and drizzle a little dressing over each.

> The old adage of oysters and an 'r' in the month still holds good even though very good farming techniques mean they are very consistent all year round. We use the Pacific variety grown around the shores of Lindisfarne Priory in Northumberland.

TIKKA SPICED MACKEREL

SERVES 2

2 mackerel, filleted

For the tikka spice
2 tablespoons oil
1 thumb size piece of ginger
1 clove of garlic
Quarter teaspoon chilli powder
1 tablespoon garam masala
1 teaspoon cumin seeds
Half teaspoon fenugreek
1 teaspoon ground turmeric

Pinch fennel seeds
Half teaspoon salt
1½ tablespoon lemon juice

For the cucumber raita
Half cucumber, seeds removed and diced
200ml natural yoghurt
1 tablespoon of fresh chopped mint
Squeeze of lemon juice
Limes to serve

METHOD

For the raita; Mix together the yoghurt, cucumber, mint and lemon juice, cover with clingfilm and place in the fridge till ready to use.

Place all the spice ingredients into a food processor and blitz to a smooth paste. Using kitchen paper, pat dry the mackerel fillets then brush each fillet generously with the tikka spice. (Any spice that is left can be covered and placed into the fridge and used within a couple of weeks.) Cover the mackerel fillet with clingfilm and place into the refrigerator for 2-3 hours to marinade.

Remove them from the fridge, heat a little oil in a large frying pan. When hot carefully lay in the fillets of mackerel, flesh side down. Cook over a moderately high heat for 3-4 minutes then turn the fillets over and cook for a further 3-4 minutes. The mackerel should feel firm to the touch. Remove the fillets from the pan onto kitchen paper to drain.

Once drained, place some salad leaves on serving plates and sit on the mackerel fillet. Spoon over some cucumber raita and finish with wedges of lime.

WHITBY CRAB LINGUINI

SERVES 4

200g brown crab meat
150g white crab meat
8 picked crab claws
300g dried linguini
2 banana shallots, finely sliced
2 cloves of garlic, crushed
1 red chilli, very finely sliced
50ml of dry sherry (Manzanilla is a good dry sherry with lots of flavour)

1 tablespoon fresh chopped marjoram or 1 teaspoon dried
1 tablespoon chives, chopped
4 spring onions, very finely sliced
Olive oil
Salt and freshly ground black pepper

METHOD

Heat a pan of salted water for the pasta and bring to the boil. Add the linguini to the boiling water and cook for the time recommended on the packet.

For the crab; Heat a little oil in a large pan and add the shallots, chilli and garlic. Over a medium heat cook until softened, then add the sherry followed by the crab. Gently heat. Once the crab is hot add the chopped herbs and then strain the pasta and add to the pan. Season with salt and freshly-ground black pepper. Toss all the ingredients together, coating all the pasta with the crab.

To serve, divide the pasta between four bowls, drizzle over olive oil and garnish with the finely-sliced spring onion and fresh herbs and accompany with freshly baked focaccia.

WHITBY CRAB PATÉ WITH PICKLED CUCUMBER

SERVES 6

500g brown crab meat
150g white crab meat
1 onion, roughly chopped
1 carrot, roughly chopped
1 stick of celery, roughly chopped
1 clove of garlic, crushed
1 tablespoon chopped tarragon
100ml white wine
250g unsalted butter
Oil for cooking
Melted butter to finish

For the pickled cucumber
1 cucumber, cut into very thin strips
1 medium onion, finely sliced
2 tablespoons salt
200ml white wine vinegar
2 tablespoon caster sugar
1 teaspoon black mustard seeds
4 cloves
Oil for cooking

METHOD

Place the cucumber and sliced onion into a bowl and sprinkle over the two tablespoons of salt. Mix well, cover and place in the fridge for a couple of hours to draw excess liquid from them. After a couple of hours, rinse the cucumber and onion well. In a pan mix together the vinegar, sugar, mustard seeds and cloves. Heat until the sugar has dissolved. Place the cucumber and onion into a jar and pour in the vinegar mix. Close the lid and leave for a minimum of 24 hours before using.

For the crab paté; Heat a little oil in a pan and fry the onion, carrot, celery and garlic. Over a medium heat cook these until soft. Add the brown crab meat and white wine and mix through. Cook for around 5 minutes then remove from the heat. Transfer the crab into a food processor and blitz until smooth, keep the food processor running and slowly adding the chilled unsalted butter a little at a time. Remove the crab from the food processor to a bowl and fold through the white crab meat and the tarragon. Taste and add seasoning if required.

Place the paté into small Kilner jars and top with a little melted butter, then place the jars into the fridge to chill and set.

Serve with a few dressed leaves, the pickled cucumber and toasted bread.

WHITBY EGGS BENEDICT

SERVES 4

2 English muffins
4 kipper fillets
6 crushed peppercorns
2 tablespoons white wine vinegar
4 egg yolks
400g clarified butter
4 eggs for poaching
Dill to garnish

METHOD

For the hollandaise; First clarify the butter by placing in a pan and gently heating, any milk solids will collect on the bottom of the pan and the clarified butter will be above.

Reduce the vinegar with the peppercorns by one-third, remove from the heat and add a tablespoon of water. Allow to cool slightly. Whisk the egg yolks over a bain-marie (water bath) to a sabayon (this is to cook the egg; it should be the consistency of thick cream). Remove from the heat and cool slightly, gradually whisking in the warm clarified butter. Do this slowly as if you add too much butter at once the sauce may split. If the sauce does split don't worry, just whisk in a little warm water. Once all the butter has been added taste and season with salt.

Place the kipper fillets into a jug and pour over boiling water, cover and let cook for 5 minutes.

Whilst the kippers are cooking poach the eggs. In a pan bring to the boil water which has been seasoned with salt and a good splash of malt vinegar. Once the water is boiling reduce the heat to a simmer and one by one add the eggs. Poach the eggs for 4 minutes.

Slice the muffins in half and toast them on both sides. Place the toasted muffins on a plate, remove the kippers from the water, drain then place the kipper onto the muffin. Remove the poached eggs from the water, drain then place on top of the kipper. Finally take the hollandaise sauce and spoon it over the eggs and finish with a sprig of dill.

WHOLE MEGRIM SOLE, BROWN SHRIMP AND WILD GARLIC BUTTER SAUCE

SERVES 4

4 whole megrim sole
8-10 sprigs of thyme
150g brown shrimp
2 shallots, sliced
1 clove of garlic, crushed
1 handful wild garlic, thinly sliced
150ml white wine
Splash of white wine vinegar

100g unsalted butter
400g part boiled potatoes, evenly sliced
1 large onion, thinly sliced
1 tablespoon parsley, chopped
Knob of butter
Oil for cooking

METHOD

Place the megrim sole onto a baking sheet and make incisions at an angle across the brown side of the fish, deep enough to reach the bone. Season with salt and pepper and drizzle with olive oil. Cover with the sprigs of thyme. Place in a preheated oven (220°C/Gas 8) for 12-15 minutes.

For the potatoes; Heat a little oil in a frying pan and add the onion. Fry over a medium heat until softened and slightly caramelised. Remove the onions from the pan and set aside. Add the potatoes to the pan with a little more oil, cook to evenly brown, turning frequently. Once the potatoes are evenly coloured add the knob of butter, parsley and season with salt and pepper. Toss the pan to mix together and then remove the potatoes from the pan onto kitchen paper to drain. Keep warm.

For the sauce; Heat a little oil in a pan and add the shallots and garlic. Saute until soft then add the white wine and vinegar. Bring to the boil and reduce a little before adding the thinly-sliced wild garlic and shrimp. Bring back to the boil and slowly add the chilled butter a little at a time, shaking the pan to incorporate it. Once all the butter has been added the sauce should be glossy and coat the back of a spoon. Do not boil the sauce as it may split.

To serve; Place a megrim sole onto each plate and spoon over the brown shrimp sauce and serve with the Lyonnaise potatoes.

WILD SEA BASS CEVICHE

SERVES 4

400g sea bass fillets, very thinly sliced
2 limes
2 red chillies, very finely sliced
Coriander leaves
Spring onions, very finely chopped
Sea salt
Flat breads to serve

For the guacamole
2 ripe avocados
1 red chilli, finely sliced
Pinch of salt
Juice of 1 lime
1 tomato, finely chopped
2 spring onions, finely sliced
1 teaspoon chopped coriander
1 tablespoon oil

METHOD

Lay the slices of sea bass evenly across a chilled plate. Finely grate the limes and then squeeze the juice from them over the sea bass. Scatter over the chilli, spring onions, coriander leaves and sea salt. Cover the sea bass and place the plate in the fridge for a couple of hours to take on the flavours.

For the guacamole; Remove the flesh from the avocados and place this into a bowl. Coarsely mash with a fork and add the juice of the lime, spring onions, chilli, tomato, coriander, salt and oil. Fold these through the avocado, taste and add more salt if required.

Serve the sea bass with warm flat breads and the guacamole.

WILD SEA TROUT CEVICHE

SERVES 4

300g fresh sea trout, very thinly-sliced
1 lemon, juice and zest
2 limes, juice and zest
1 teaspoon caster sugar
1 tablespoon coriander, finely chopped
1 tablespoon miniature capers
4 pickled onions, very finely sliced
Sea salt
Black pepper

For the pomegranate and feta salad
1 pomegranate
150g feta cheese, diced
Handful of watercress
Drizzle of olive oil
Splash of sherry vinegar
1 tablespoon of toasted pine nuts

METHOD

Lay the sea trout evenly across a large plate. In a bowl mix together the juice and zest of the lemon, limes, caster sugar, coriander, capers and spring onions. Once mixed and the sugar has dissolved, spoon evenly over the trout. Cover with clingfilm and place into the fridge for at least 6 hours. Just before serving, sprinkle over sea salt and freshly-milled black pepper.

For the salad; Bash the seeds out of the pomegranate (using the back of a spoon) into a bowl and add the oil, vinegar and pine nuts. Toss to mix together. Place the watercress in a bowl and drop over the feta cheese then spoon over the pomegranate mix.

Serve the salad with the sea trout and plenty of freshly-baked bread.

WOOF WITH 'PASTA PUTTANESCA'

SERVES 2

2 x 200g woof fillets
1 good handful (200g) of linguini
200ml passata
1 tablespoon tomato purée
2 cloves of garlic, sliced
1 tablespoon of stoneless black olives, split in half

1 teaspoon dried chilli flakes
6 anchovy fillets (tinned variety)
1 tablespoon capers, roughly chopped
1 tablespoon parsley, chopped
Olive oil for cooking
Salt and pepper

METHOD

For the sauce; Heat a little oil in a pan and add the sliced garlic. Cook gently over a low heat until softened. Fry the anchovies, chilli flakes and capers, then after a minute add the tomato purée, passata and olives. Bring to the boil and reduce the heat to a simmer. Cook for around 30 minutes on a very low heat. Finish with the chopped parsley.

For the woof; Season the fish with salt and pepper and seal over quite a high heat, turning occasionally. Transfer the woof to a preheated hot oven for around 8 minutes.

Cook the pasta as the packet describes. Drain off any excess water and add the pasta to the sauce, tossing vigorously to combine. Divide the pasta between two bowls and put the woof on top. Finish with basil leaves and a drizzle of olive oil.

FISH & SHIPS

Yes, you read it correctly. Everyone knows the Magpie Café for its famous fish and chips. But there was a surprise in store when visitors to Whitby were treated to an altogether new experience – two days of Fish and Ships.

The occasion was a festival celebrating all that's best about seafood from North Yorkshire's coast, as well as the fishing industry. The Ships came in the shape of vessels under construction at one of the UK's most successful boatbuilders, Parkol Marine Engineering. It gave visitors an unprecedented opportunity to explore the shipyard and dry dock. Also on show were all types of marine craft. Crowds gathered to see the trawler Success 111 landing fish live in Whitby, while the free tours of the North Eastern Guardian 111 provided a unique opportunity to look around this state-of-the-art patrol/research vessel.

A full programme of events which included everything from demonstrations by local fishermen to live maritime music and rowing races ensured there was something for everyone. But the festival was above all about the food which the industry supplies, in all its variety. So it was particularly pleasing to see an old friend of the Magpie, television chef Brian Turner CBE, doing live cookery demonstrations to inspire home cooks with seafood treats.

Word is that the success of the festival will mean it will become an annual event. Don't miss out!

THANKS

I would like to dedicate this book to all those who helped us through the traumatic aftermath of the disastrous fire of May 2017.

Particular thanks to Arnold and Sheila at Lockers Fish, Sheila McKenzie and not forgetting our loyal staff who stayed with us through the dark days.

Our heartfelt thanks also go to Brian Turner CBE for once again generously providing the foreword for this, our third book.

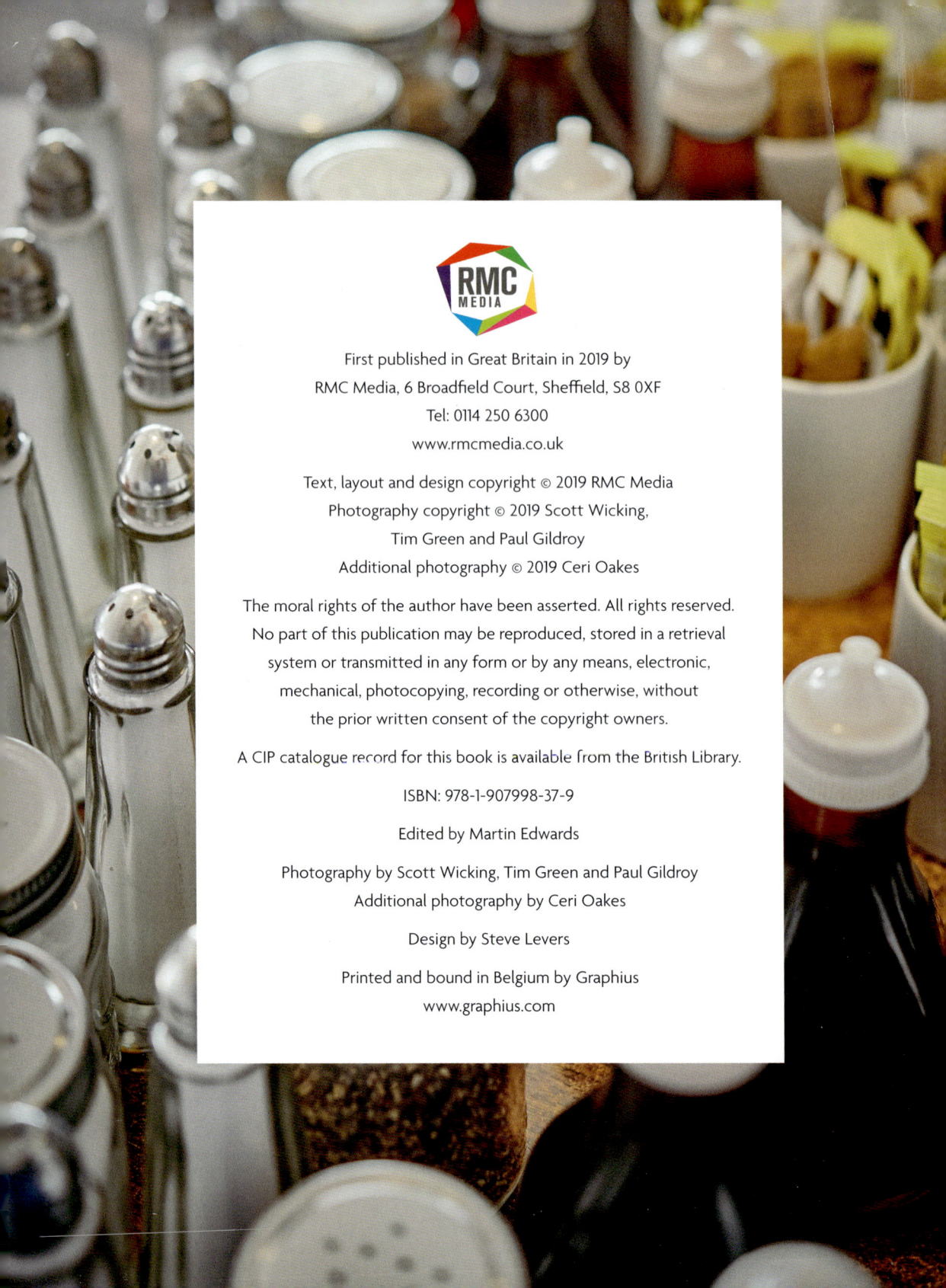

First published in Great Britain in 2019 by
RMC Media, 6 Broadfield Court, Sheffield, S8 0XF
Tel: 0114 250 6300
www.rmcmedia.co.uk

Text, layout and design copyright © 2019 RMC Media
Photography copyright © 2019 Scott Wicking,
Tim Green and Paul Gildroy
Additional photography © 2019 Ceri Oakes

The moral rights of the author have been asserted. All rights reserved. No part of this publication may be reproduced, stored in a retrieval system or transmitted in any form or by any means, electronic, mechanical, photocopying, recording or otherwise, without the prior written consent of the copyright owners.

A CIP catalogue record for this book is available from the British Library.

ISBN: 978-1-907998-37-9

Edited by Martin Edwards

Photography by Scott Wicking, Tim Green and Paul Gildroy
Additional photography by Ceri Oakes

Design by Steve Levers

Printed and bound in Belgium by Graphius
www.graphius.com